THE CONVOY

Also by Beata Umubyeyi Mairesse in English translation
All Your Children, Scattered

Beata Umubyeyi Mairesse

THE CONVOY

*Translated from the French by
Ruth Diver*

OPEN BORDERS PRESS
LONDON

Published in Great Britain in 2025 by
Open Borders Press
an imprint of
Orenda Books
London
www.openborderspress.co.uk

9 8 7 6 5 4 3 2 1

Originally published in France as *Le Convoi*
© Flammarion, 2024 pour l'édition en langue française
© Beata Umubyeyi Mairesse, 2024
Translation © Ruth Diver, 2025

The moral right of Beata Umubyeyi Mairesse to be recognised as
the author of this work has been asserted in accordance with the
Copyright, Designs and Patents Act, 1988

Ruth Diver asserts her moral right to be identified as
the translator of this work

*Cet ouvrage a bénéficié du soutien des Programmes d'aide
à la publication de l'Institut français*

The publisher acknowledges the use of e-mails sent to the author by Mark Doyle, Fergal Keane, Milton Nkosi and Alice Doyard and extracts from "A Litany for Survival" by Audre Lorde (*The Black Unicorn*, published by Penguin. Copyright © Audre Lorde. Reprinted with permission), *Rwanda, entre crise morale et malaise esthétique – Les médias, la photographie et le cinéma à l'épreuve du génocide des Tutsi (1994–2014)* by Nathan Réra (Les Presses du réel, 2014), *Regarding the Pain of Others* by Susan Sontag (published by Penguin. Copyright © Susan Sontag, 2003. Reprinted by permission of Penguin Books Limited) and *Season of Blood: A Rwandan Journey* by Fergal Keane (Penguin, 1994) with kind permission of the author.

All rights reserved. No part of this publication may be reproduced, stored in any retrieval system, or transmitted in any form or by any means, electronically, mechanical, photocopying, recording or otherwise, without the prior permission of the copyright owners and the publishers

A CIP catalogue record for this book is available from the British Library

ISBN (HB) 978-1-916788-70-1

Map © Emily Faccini

Designed and typeset in Sabon by Libanus Press
Printed and bound in Great Britain by CPI Group (UK) Ltd, Croydon, CR0 4YY

The author acknowledges the *Fondation des Treilles* (Var)
for the writing residency of two months which
it awarded her in 2022.
The aims and objectives of the *Fondation des Treilles*,
created by Anne Gruner Schlumberger,
are to foster dialogue between science and the arts
in order to advance creativity and research.
www.les-treilles.com

CONTENTS

Map	10–11
Prologue	15
Part I: Four Photographs	33
Part II: The Tense of Testimony	73
Part III: *Terre des Hommes*	137
Part IV: Our Time Has Come	197
Epilogue	256
Notes	269
Chronology	271
Acknowledgements	275
Sources	276
Index	279

For Mfurayanjye, who is now fifteen years old.
And for Micomyiza, who will be one day.

"This child who says he is alive and is telling the tale, that's me. In the middle of life, childhood returns, sweet and bitter, with its pictures."

Rithy Pahn and Christophe Bataille
The Missing Picture

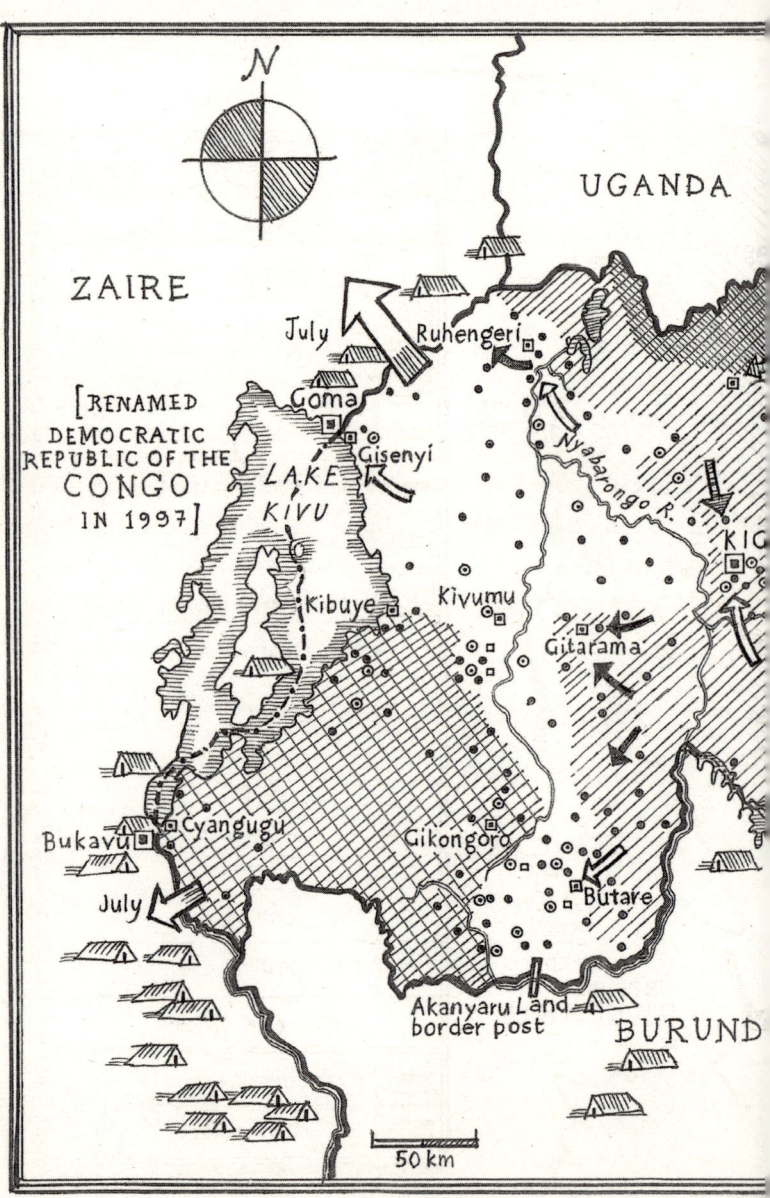

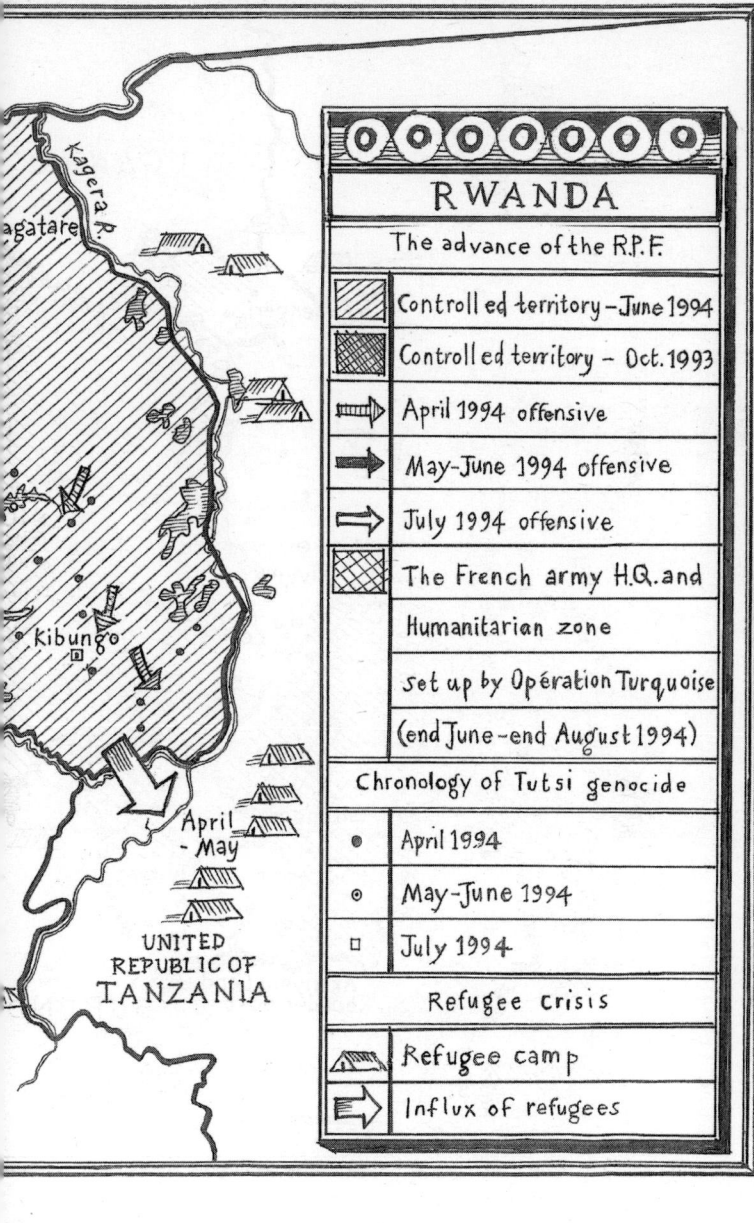

My life was spared. On June 18, 1994, a few weeks before the end of the genocide against the Tutsi, I was able to flee my country thanks to a convoy organised by the Swiss humanitarian agency *Terre des Hommes*. I was fifteen years old at the time. The rescue operation was officially reserved for children aged under twelve, but my mother and I were able to be included in it, hidden in the back of a container truck. During the following weeks, some people told us that they saw us on television as we were crossing the border between Rwanda and Burundi, a crossing we undertook on foot.

In 2007 I contacted the B.B.C. crew that had filmed our convoy, in the hope of getting a copy of the video in which I appeared. I have not been able to find that footage.

One of the journalists gave me four photographs that he had taken that day. I could not see myself in them. At the time, I had no idea what to do with those images.

On August 18, 2020, I found the humanitarian aid worker who had organised our rescue in 1994.

He died four months later.

That is when I decided to write this story.

Prologue

It would take an uncertain journey of fifteen years, an investigation of the depths of fading memories, to find an image in which I hoped I might appear, then to search for my companions in flight, then at last to explore the possibility of weaving together an account that people would be willing to hear. Fifteen years to allow myself to write this story at last. My own story, and through it – for this is really about finding my place within a community once again – ours, the story of the children of the convoys.

This word "convoy" is freighted with a terrible meaning in the society from which I am now speaking. This society that generously welcomed me, at a time when that still seemed the natural thing to do, with no other condition but to leave the past behind me, at the furthest reaches of Western consciences, as one accepts shedding a skin, but as a silencing nevertheless. Here in France people think about death convoys, about the trains that took away the victims of another genocide, fifty years before ours, towards the concentration and extermination camps which so few survived. It was through reading the words of those who did return, through learning to journey alongside them, that I forged the language that now allows me to tell the story of other convoys. Those of my people, the one thanks to which I survived, in Rwanda, on June 18, 1994.

A convoy to life.

*

Launching into this account today demands that I consider my past as honestly as possible, that I rediscover who I was back then.

An adolescent, wrenched out of childhood by men's violence, crosses a border thanks to a rescue operation led by humanitarian aid workers. She escapes death in improbable circumstances, but at that moment she has no idea that she will one day turn this into any kind of story. She is unaware at the time that *Terre des Hommes*, the name of the N.G.O. that ensured her safe passage, is also the title of a book by Antoine de Saint-Exupéry, published on the eve of World War II. She registers the scenes, but especially imprints the sensations, the few words spoken, and the mute terror too. She clings to the hope of life, this new, fragile and uncertain life, which is revealing itself on the other side of the bridge she is about to cross to leave her country. In the weeks that follow, she will cross other borders; the horizon will open up to offer her a protected existence in a foreign land. Much more than a passport or a visa, it is a language, French, that allows her to cross all these borders symbolically and physically. A language as a shield that she used to drive away the killers, that she is still using to conquer the new territory in which she must find her feet: France. As the months go by, her vocabulary in this language which she mastered as a child becomes filled with new words: "genocide", "rescue", "survivor". Those words she had read in histories of times that were said to be past. She will try to make them her own. She must, for she understands that the world is constantly using them to describe her experience in that country she was able to flee. Those words are stamped on all the pages of the immaterial passport that she must present, as a foreigner, as she enters the new life she now must build. She discovers that what happened in that country and what took most of her loved ones from her, those events, of which she still retains a vivid memory, are defined by this word: genocide. It is a huge word that crushes her, but also a tiny word that can never contain the extent of her loss. One that does not speak the names of the dead, her two cousins, Uwingabire and Mpinganzima, with whom she used to play, or her second cousin nicknamed "Captain", or the names of her uncle and aunt, or of all the others, of all her extended family. It says nothing of the friends and neighbours, of the dozens of people whose names, like constellations, had always marked the expanse of a plural existence, of an "us" that was suddenly erased.

That word should summarise everything, and now, in fact, in the language of those around her, in the minimalist account they give to introduce her – as the new pupil at school, the little refugee – it is often enough, along with the name of her country, to impose silence. A blank moment of embarrassment and compassion, in which there is no room to unravel the past in all its complexity. She quickly understands that in this land of opulence and peace, she must also learn to keep quiet. She who had always dreamed of becoming a journalist discovers that liberty of expression may well be a reality here, but it is one that is circumscribed. "Rwanda" and "genocide" – those two words take up all the available space, and the first one doesn't even seem to need the second. In the minds of French people, most of whom had never even heard that word until it crept into their newspapers, "Rwanda" has become synonymous with horror and violence. It also evokes "interethnic massacres" and "tribal barbarity". Everything is mixed up. People are in the habit of simplifying things when it comes to Africa. Rwanda is all the proof that is required that the caricatural image of the "heart of darkness", that Conradian expression that has been a catch-phrase since colonial times, can still be used without compunction.

Even though Africa has rid itself of some of its demons, there will always be some part of that darkness that will rear up again: apartheid is over, of course, but then look at Rwanda.

For those people, that's the way it is. And always has been.

No-one wants to hear the rare voices reminding them that the ethnicisation of Rwandan society is a colonial construct. It's just that they've been killing each other since the dawn of time, haven't they?

Come to think of it, there are three words: anyone who says "Rwanda" also evokes "machete", which itself evokes "genocide". Three words unendingly contaminating each other in macabre causality, stifling the unfurling of any individual, circumstantial narrative, of any story of one's own. The fear of specific details, of any expression of personal experience, jams the airwaves. And in any case, most people have already seen far too much on television over the past months to want to hear anything more about all that from the adolescent girl being introduced to them. Or perhaps they fear that madness might engulf her if she starts bringing out her dead in front of them – as the rivers of Rwanda did, washing corpses into the lakes of neighbouring countries, also shown on the world's television screens – this madness from which she needs to be protected, which needs to be circumscribed in the past, in that other place. In the meantime, she quickly learns how to behave in France and decides to adopt the resilience programme that French society has devised for children like her. It has not yet become the global injunction that we hear about today, the one where polluted nature, raped women and shipwrecked migrants must all show resilience. But from the moment she is offered the support of care, education and security, she cannot continue to talk about the past without showing herself to be ungrateful.

PROLOGUE

In the Catholic *lycée* of Beaucamps-Ligny, near Lille, which enrols her for free thanks to a programme for the education of children from war-torn countries – such as the Lebanese pupils before her – she learns quickly. And when someone asks her how she is getting on now, she knows she must answer: "Very well, thank you. The past is the past."

And so here I am now, thirty years later, deciding to turn back to that past and to write about it. What exactly happened?

I arrived in the north of France at the age of fifteen. I had not been raped, nor hacked with a machete, and I still had by my side my loving mother, who had survived along with me. My mother very quickly returned to Rwanda to look for other survivors, to be with them, leaving me in the care of a wonderful French host family, with whom I had the opportunity of starting my life all over again from where genocide had left it.

My host family offered me not only affection and room and board, they also helped me to salve my sorrow by opening the doors of psychotherapy to me.

My life became almost normal again, as if by magic.

The only narrative that I allowed myself for two decades was the one that I unfolded in the consulting rooms of psychologists and psychiatrists – where I would find myself exploring much more than my experience of survival – or in conversations with the very few people who dared to ask me: "What happened to you?"

For everyone else, for my friends, teachers or colleagues, I became this woman who, thanks to her work and humanitarian activities, had managed to give back to the world some of the help she received as an adolescent. When I started out in my working life, I chose to get involved in symbolic battles against death: combating A.I.D.S., addictions, suicide.

The years passed.

I avidly read whatever was published about Rwanda, essays written by journalists or historians, and the first testimonies by Tutsi survivors. I also found words in the accounts of Holocaust survivors that had the exact shape of my loneliness. Thanks to those words, I was able to tame my silence.

One day, at the very end of the century, as I was sensing that my memory was already starting to crumble, I jotted down in a little spiral-bound notebook a few dates, a few facts from those months of April to June 1994 that my mother and I had endured in hiding or on the run. My thinking was that, should I one day become a mother myself, my children might well ask me to tell them about that time.

Sometimes a journalist or an acquaintance would ask me to tell them about my experience so that they could write it up and publish it. I always declined, already confusedly aware that if my story were ever to be told, I would want it to be in my own words.

I fell in love with a young Frenchman who was not afraid of knowing. He asked me to tell him my story very soon after we met. As the years went by, he also gleaned a few of my memories that found their way unbidden into our daily conversations.

When we were expecting our first child, Yann, who had become my husband, suggested that we go in search of the images that I had told him about. Some people, whose identity I have now forgotten (maybe some friends we found in Burundi in June 1994, or in France shortly afterwards, people who had cable T.V.?), had said that they saw us on British television, my mother and I, as we were crossing the border between Rwanda and Burundi, on the day we escaped.

That is how the investigation that would lead to this book started, in 2007.

But books had come into the picture much earlier.

At thirty years old, I came across this sentence by Toni Morrison: "If there's a book that you want to read, but it has not been written yet, then you must write it." I realised that through all those years of silence and my attempts at "exemplary resilience", I had been looking for the book that I could give to those who, despite their closeness and goodwill, gave me the impression of not being ready to read a first-hand account, mine or anyone else's. Something to read for people who kept repeating that it was "indescribable" without really thinking it through. What I realised is that words can indeed contain the scope of the disaster – eyewitness accounts are there to prove it – and that our inability to communicate actually stems from the fact that those words are inaudible. I wanted to write something that would recount the experience of survival, both here and back there, in all its multiformity and over the long term, without resorting to euphemisms, but also without it being frightening. Something that would describe the before and the after in order to explain the three months of night that we endured. I understood that it would take painstaking craftsmanship to make our stories acceptable, even though the crimes were not. And so I launched myself into writing my first collection of short stories, which I titled *Ejo*,[1] a word that means both "yesterday" and "tomorrow" in the language of the country of my birth. I chose fiction as a way of keeping a necessary distance, for myself and for my readers. Some of the stories were inspired by real events or people I had transformed in my imagination.

This was followed by another collection of short stories and a novel that, in one way or another, made it possible to understand how lives were stopped, ravaged and forever changed by the genocide.

Those books were read by the people they were intended for and by many others as well. Often French readers would talk about them using words like "your testimony", and no matter how much I might protest that this was not my personal story, I understood how difficult it would be for me to extract myself from this framework in which works of fiction from Africa are so often considered as ethnographical treatises.

Rwandan men and women also read my work, and I was glad to hear their enthusiastic reactions. A playwright friend of mine, for example, wrote: "Thanks to your novel I am rediscovering my whole city of Butare, which you have resurrected, it's fabulous." An acquaintance, an older person, thanked me for having "so beautifully brought our finest proverbs to the fore". My mixed race, which gave me the impression as a child of being always set apart by a difference that was too visible, had given me a complex of not belonging. I thought that, after 1994, the extreme experience of genocide, which I had endured alongside everyone else, would at last authorise me to be completely Rwandan.

That remained fragile, however. I would be invited to talk about my books, and congratulated for my knowledge of our language, Kinyarwanda, to which I gave a prominent place in my literary works. And yet.

One day, the head of a survivors' advocacy group told me, as part of an invitation to speak to a school class about the genocide against the Tutsi: "There will be a survivor and yourself." I do not know whether he made this distinction because I had been invited to talk not only about my experience in 1994, but also about my books. Am I not a survivor just as the others are? I did not dare ask.

In the Western world of creative writing that I entered with my first books, and despite the acclaim from critics and booksellers, all it took was a few cuts to make me falter.

An editor with whom I was supposed to work told me one day, I imagine without thinking too much about it, that it would be difficult for her to promote my work because "that niche is already taken". And when I asked her, incredulously, what she meant by that, she explained that there was already a Rwandan woman writer in the publishing landscape. I could not believe my ears. Do I not have the right to be an author too, just because I am also Rwandan? Are we still at the point of thinking, in Paris, that there is only one place, one voice, per African country, and that we must compete to win it? I was mortified.

A few months later, a dear friend, an author who had worked for a long time – and with much talent – with Rwandan stories, asked me in front of the audience of a talk we were giving: "Why do the bios on your books all say that you are a survivor? Is that your occupation?"

This question would be offensive for anyone, but it was all the more so for me, in that it came on the heels of those other situations I just mentioned, which I experienced as negations. I reminded him, since I felt he was demanding that I justify myself, of the cases of other Rwandan writers who had been presented as survivors of the genocide when they in fact were not. Why should I then not have the right to say that it is from my real, lived experience that I write?

*

I was discouraged for a time and considered never writing this story. But silence, as I learned from reading Audre Lorde, would not bring me peace:

> [. . .]
> and when we speak we are afraid
> our words will not be heard
> nor welcomed
> but when we are silent
> we are still afraid
>
> So it is better to speak
> remembering
> we were never meant to survive.

And so, for years, and maybe this still holds true today, I was hampered by the paradoxical attributions and injunctions of others, to which I had no idea how to respond.

Now at the end of my journey between memory and writing, I understand that I will carry this fragility for a long time. I know there will always be someone to tell me that my tale has already been told, and at the same time, in a dizzying contradiction, someone else to tell me that it is too personal, not "universal" enough. I know that there will be people to tell me I am exaggerating, that I am too hard, or that I did not understand them. But did they ever try to understand me?

Writing this book has been a constant balancing act. I must tell this story. Can I do it alone, can I grant myself that right? Who am I to do so? A survivor, to be sure, but a privileged survivor, since my lighter-coloured skin allowed me to be spared the fate that so many others met. A writer, yes, but one who until now has stayed safely retrenched in the comfort of fiction, and has carefully avoided revealing her naked life.

How am I to pass from fiction to the portrayal of real events, how can I tame the narrative of historical facts in which I am a protagonist?

In an interview in 1986, Primo Levi recounts how he went from writing autobiography to his first novel, *If Not Now, When?*, a story of Polish and Russian Jewish partisans attacking the Nazis behind the Eastern Front during the last two years of the war. He says that he set himself the challenge of finding out whether or not he had become "a fully-fledged writer, capable of constructing a novel, shaping character, describing landscapes [he had] never seen".

Without wishing to compare myself to such a foundational author as Primo Levi, but because I could not help looking for answers in his work – and in that of Charlotte Delbo and Aharon Appelfeld – it occurred to me on reading those lines that I was taking a path in the opposite direction. Going from fiction to personal account to prove to myself . . . what, exactly?

That I have the right to be a survivor just like the others?

Not a day goes by when I do not doubt that. Am I on the right path? I would like to find the other children of the convoy of June 18, to give them the photographs, to give them this story. Will they find my work useful? Might they feel as if I have appropriated this story that is also theirs? Would it not be better for me to stop saying "I" and just to write the story of our crossing, as a journalistic account, from an outside perspective? And what about the journalists who were there? Won't they find my comments about them unjust or presumptuous?

For I was only a child in 1994 and it would seem logical that it should be the adults who tell that story. Some of them have done so, and their accounts have fed into my own. These are the foreign men, journalists or rescuers, who left a written trace in books, articles or documentary films. A humanitarian aid worker and a journalist were witnesses at the International Criminal Tribunal for Rwanda (I.C.T.R.), which recorded all of their words.

The women and children, with the exception of one single survivor, my friend Annick Kayitesi-Jozan, have remained silent. And this has bolstered my determination: to make space, finally, for their words in this account, which must become a collective one. To write from those identities, past and present, from the child I was and the woman I have become.

I often doubted myself. But if I abandoned the project, I feared this story might be told by someone who could not tell it from the inside as I would. I feared that he or she would not be troubled by the questions of legitimacy that I was asking myself, that he or she might lack distance, or perhaps delicacy. Were my doubts a surfeit of delicacy? I would not want anyone else to turn us into a caricature or a fine story, or to speak in our place. But then what should I do in order not to be charged with wanting to tell "a fine story" or speaking in the place of others? I realised very quickly that I would never be able to include all the memories, those of others as well as my own, to carry us all singlehandedly, to carry us all in words. My own memory has frayed a little, it is full of holes which I have no way of mending, but which I nevertheless must not hide.

Another fear welled up, as I was writing the first pages: someone is bound to say that my version of the facts does not conform to *the* truth. I remembered a scene that someone had told me about, of a Holocaust survivor who was speaking to a class of schoolchildren, and of another survivor who was in the room, who had told the person sitting next to her (the one who told me this story): "She is talking nonsense, that's not how it happened at all!" Our memories are defective, reconstituted, dissonant.

I started, again and again, then I stopped. It was not writer's block but the fear of not being the right chronicler, of not creating an irreproachable account, one faithful to the facts and to the victims, one that would deal kindly with the contradictions of those who helped us or told our story.

In order to reassure myself, I often think about the words of some of the journalists who were present at the border the day we crossed in 1994, whom I found again and to whom I entrusted my project: "It's up to you to write this story. You are doing the right thing. You are the only person who can do it."

To begin with, I was looking for a list of names. Those of the children in the convoy of June 18, with whom I wanted to share four photographs that I had found, and to restore a little of our common past.

Except that, as the years went by, instead of leading me to the names of survivors, my investigation mostly brought me the names of the rescuers, the witnesses and the killers, the only ones which were recorded in writing and in the archives. The rescued children remained an undifferentiated mass for a long time. As if our lives had left no trace, as if we were condemned to remain children indefinitely, those who gave others their roles, who turned others into rescuers, witnesses, accomplices or killers.

Should I continue to look for the children? I realise that what I have to offer may be a disappointment for them. A few photographs, some dates and the destiny of our rescuers. Even if there are only a handful of them, some of them could read this story, in this generation or the next. The children of 1994 no doubt have children of their own by now, and those photographs, in a family album of the past, might present a possibility of telling the story of their survival, of weaving together the threads of frayed memories.

Since I started writing, my reading and my encounters have shifted some of my convictions. For instance, I did not think, at the start, that I would write my own first-hand account, tell the story of what I had endured myself before I reached the *Terre des Hommes* centre. And then I went and talked to a *lycée* class and, when I got home, as I sat back down at my desk, it seemed unthinkable that I should not do so. I could not talk about the other children, give an account of the few lives that I had been able to find again, and excise myself from the story. Recounting my experience in the convoy would only make sense if I took the trouble to talk about the weeks preceding it, weeks of hiding and fear that had led me to the location set up by the N.G.O.

In the same way, the question of the form of the account slowly evolved.

The writers Daniel Mendelsohn and Imre Kertész taught me that the way one tells a story is just as important as what one decides to share. I had imagined that I would shed the novelist's cloak for this book, and become nothing more than a witness, just like the others. I did not want to "create literature" with our story, but I could not stop wondering whether I might not have to succumb to that imperative. For if I contented myself with a linear narrative, if I restricted myself to the factual account of what happened to us from April to June 1994, no-one would know anything about what time does to the past. It amplifies, erodes or cracks it into fragments, into pebbles that are scattered or stay still, lost on the side of the path, but which can be found again when the time of telling arrives. Then the old and the new, the life of before and the life of afterwards, resonate together and make sense.

Those fragments are assembled here into a mosaic that has more to show than the convoy of June 18. Only if I tell the story of my fifteen-year quest along the winding pathways of memories spread over Rwanda, England, Italy, Switzerland, France and South Africa can the dizzying odds of that escape and the meaning of that particular day be understood.

*

Sometimes you have to tell one story to reach another one. Each story holds other stories, and by writing in spirals, I am not scattering myself but moving forward. For I must continue, I must say all the words while they are still there. Say everything before I forget it.

Adding individual stories to the central story of the convoy is also a way for me to widen the horizon of the world I am writing about, of the event that I am describing, to show how it echoes with the present and with other worlds. A way to show its many layers. Each one of the children is much more than a human life that was destroyed or saved; each of the protagonists of that inaugural scene between Rwanda and Burundi, on June 18, 1994, can bear witness to a journey of thirty years on the borders of fragile humanity, to a life story thrown off course.

On June 18, 1994, a few weeks before the end of the genocide against the Tutsi, I flee my country thanks to a convoy organised by the humanitarian agency *Terre des Hommes*. I am fifteen years old. The rescue operation is officially reserved for children under twelve, but my mother and I are part of it, hidden in the back of a container truck. In the following days, some people tell us that they saw us on the B.B.C. as we were crossing the border between Rwanda and Burundi. More than ten years after the events, I contact the British television crew that filmed our convoy, in the hope of getting a copy of the footage in which I appear. I do not manage to find those images of me. One of the journalists sends me four photographs. I do not find myself in them and at the time I have no idea what to do with them.

I file them in a folder on my computer and assume I will forget them.

I

Four Photographs

". . . only then did I know beyond any doubt that these fragments of memory were part of my own life as well. I was too alarmed by this sudden revelation to be able to write down the addresses and phone numbers given at the end of the programme. I merely saw myself waiting on a quay in a long crocodile of children lined up two by two, most of them carrying rucksacks or small leather cases."

Austerlitz
W.G. Sebald
Translated by Anthea Bell

Nice, spring 2019

I was participating in the annual Memory Week organised by the *Lycée Thierry-Maulnier* in Nice for the fourth year running.

All year long, the five wonderful teachers who were responsible for this project would have their students working on the genocides of the Jews, the Tutsi and the Armenians. Then they organised a week of presentations by researchers, therapists, artists and survivors or their descendants.

This pedagogical and human approach aimed not only to provide information, but also to sow a few seeds in the young people that, as they germinated, might allow them to become vigilant and engaged citizens, able to carry forward memory.

It was in this school, in front of adolescents of fifteen, the same age I was in 1994, that I first started bearing witness to my experience as a writer and survivor. I could see myself in them, and my writing, which their French teacher had assigned them to read, was all the more meaningful to them since it was by a direct witness of the genocide.

The first time I participated, in 2016, I was profoundly moved by the presentation of Evelyn Askolovitch, who had survived the Holocaust as a child with her mother and father, first in two camps in Holland, then at Bergen-Belsen in Germany. She talked about how for many years her mother had taken over the family memory, on the assumption that her little girl remembered nothing of those events. Which was not in fact the case, but the child had buried her own memories and remained silent, letting the adults speak, then for decades she lived in the shadow of her husband, who was a well-known journalist in the French Jewish press. It was only after her husband's death, when her mother was by now very old and she herself was almost eighty, that Evelyn finally allowed herself to speak. She had continued to do so ever since, especially in schools. As I listened to this inspiring woman tell her life story to the attentive adolescents, I had something of a bewildering realisation, which I told her about later: does this mean that I too will still have to keep speaking about my life when I am in my seventies? In her glowing eyes I saw encouragement. She herself had started speaking "late in life", and still had lots of energy for it; I was still young and would have to hold the distance and sometimes think about protecting myself.

Since that conversation with Evelyn Askolovitch, I always think about her when I talk about the Holocaust to schoolchildren. For I do take care to mention the other genocides when I present my life story to them, because of the common destiny that links me to those other survivors, and because I fundamentally trust the convergence of memories rather than their opposition, from one generation to the next.

In 2019, in Nice, I found two Rwandan survivors, Félicité Lyamukuru, the president at the time of the organisation Ibuka Belgique, and the singer Jean de Dieu Rwamihare, nicknamed "Bonhomme", who was well known in Rwanda for the heart-wrenching songs that he composed and performed during commemorations. There were also some people there devoted to the memory of other genocides, Jewish or Armenian elders who for years had been weaving the necessary connections between our respective stories, as well as the representatives of the association Ibuka France,[2] and others besides.

That evening, we attended the performance of a play, "Basculement, Rwanda 94", which was about the beginning of the genocide in Kigali. Two of the actors were themselves survivors. It was the first time I had met them. At the Q. & A. on stage after the performance, the one called Rodrigue confided some of his story to the audience. He said he escaped the massacres by leaving the country thanks to a convoy organised by the Swiss N.G.O. *Terre des Hommes*. My heart started pounding so wildly in my chest, resounding all the way into my ears, that I heard nothing more of the conversation in the theatre.

I went and waited for Rodrigue at the exit to the dressing rooms, and he was no doubt surprised by my excitement as I began to talk to him.

Today, with hindsight, I can clearly reconstitute the meaning of the words that I blurted out at him that evening, as I gesticulated and struggled for breath, but it must all have seemed quite confused to him.

"I am also a survivor from Butare. And just like you I was able to leave the country thanks to a convoy organised by *Terre des Hommes*. A few years ago, I did some research to find pictures of our convoy, because people had told us that they had seen my mother and me on television, as we were crossing the border. I found the B.B.C. journalists who filmed the rescue operation. I did not appear on any of the images that they were able to give me, but since then I have come into possession of four photographs in which you can see several children who escaped that day. Maybe you are one of them! Do you remember the date when you left? I was in the convoy on June 18, what about you?"

I did not ask Rodrigue whether or not he wanted those photographs, whether he was interested in seeing them at all, no, I imposed them on him, starting from the principle that if I had tried to find a trace of that miraculous survival, then all the other children must have done the same.

Rodrigue listened to me calmly. At the end of my long tirade, he said in a slow and measured voice that he did not remember the date of his convoy. He had been only four years old. He would ask his older cousin, who was with him on the journey.

The possibility of finding a photograph of himself during the genocide seemed to interest him, but it did not seem to hold the same importance that it held for me. I kept hurtling on and awkwardly apologised: "I've had those photos for almost ten years, and I never thought of looking for the children who are on them to give them the images. Do you realise, you and your cousin could be on them, and that memento, which is so important for you, is just sleeping in my computer."

He politely gave me the e-mail address I requested of him and promised to get any information he could.

That same evening, without even waiting for his confirmation of the date he escaped from Rwanda, I sent him the four photographs, as I would do several times subsequently, sharing those images of strangers, perhaps hoping that those four photographs might create a bond between us or speak of us as an entity that had endured through time – "the children of the convoys" – while also wondering at that moment whether I might be the only one to believe in that "entity".

Two days later, Rodrigue replied: he and his cousin Abdul were in the convoy of July 3. He added: "If you find any other photographs, do send them to me so I can have a look."

I have often thought about that conversation since then. I have tried to make sense of the young man's apparently lukewarm attitude. Was his reaction due to the fact that I was talking to him about events from his earliest childhood, about a precise moment in time of which he had no memories, whereas I have been able to recall so many details of that particular day because I was fifteen? Or was it because he had experienced much more significant things, his separation from his parents, the constant death threats, or even more terrible events? If only I could have given him a photograph of his lost family members ...

Rodrigue's reaction unsettled me. It forced me to accept the idea that not everyone accorded the same importance to those photographs as I did, given that I had been exploring the question of memory for more than a decade.

Paradoxically, this encounter became a catalyst for me: I decided to find the children that are identifiable on the four photographs, so I could give them the images. Even if the images were of interest to only one of them, I told myself, it would be worth it.

Those photographs, that story that I am attempting to reconstitute, show what has connected us since 1994: a community of experience. They are the proof that on that day, at that precise place in the country which then had the highest percentage of killers per capita in the world, we had managed to escape them one last time, thus becoming survivors.

The very fact that they exist is significant, that they will always be available to anyone who might feel the need to look at them one day, when their time comes. That is what Rodrigue and other children after him have told me, showing that very Rwandan restraint that can sometimes appear to be indifference: "If you find other photographs, do send them to me so I can have a look."

I came to understand that those images I had kept in my

possession for so long without doing anything with them are precious. And yet, when I first received them, I was almost disappointed. I was looking for a trace of myself, but I was not anywhere to be seen. Had I been in the same frame of mind as Rodrigue was when I met him?

In order to know this for sure, I need to go back to the moment when they came into my possession.

This is how everything started.

Bordeaux and London, autumn 2007

I was pregnant. My husband and I knew that this first child would be a boy. I welcomed this desired pregnancy with a serenity I did not know I was capable of. A few years earlier, reading *Kaddish for an Unborn Child* by Imre Kertész had plunged me into deep distress. This sombre and oppressive soliloquy by the Hungarian author had led me for the first time to consider the question of parenthood after a genocide. What meaning could such a decision have, to bring a human life into a world of whose inhumanity I was only too aware? Kertész survived Auschwitz at the same age I was in 1994, the same age as my friend and survivor Annick Kayitesi-Jozan, who had told me about this writer. Annick, whom I always called by her pretty childhood nickname, Zouzou, is another child of the convoys: she was part of the July one. She was the first to write her story. Her son was born within a few months of my first child. We had often lost track of each other then found each other again over the years.

While Kertész made the choice not to become a father, Annick and I followed another path. And while I had been gripped by relentless uncertainty before my pregnancy, this disappeared as soon as I knew I was going to become a mother. That was when I had the conviction, without knowing where it came from, that one can survive survival and weave a new relationship of trust with the world. I also made the resolution at that time to do everything I could to protect my son from any transmission of my trauma, not by imposing silence – which I knew would resolve nothing – but, on the contrary, by telling him my story bit by bit, according to how much his child's heart could contain and comprehend.

In the autumn of 2007, I was working for *Aides*, a charity fighting against A.I.D.S. My role was, among other things, to facilitate a discussion group of seropositive women, most of whom had been contaminated in the early 1990s and survived that terrible time before triple therapy was available. Their words and gestures around my swelling belly were so sweet. Some of them had unknowingly transmitted the virus to their children, who were then living fragile, constantly medicated lives. Others, the younger ones, hoped to be allowed to get pregnant one day without the risk of contamination that the medical establishment still presented as an obstacle.

I understand today that it was probably the fact that I was going to become a mother which made me decide to start this search.

I was four months pregnant when I agreed to let my husband contact the B.B.C. I had told him the story of the people who said they had seen us, my mother and me, in a report broadcast in June 1994. It was a vague memory to which I had never accorded much importance, unlike my husband, who had mentioned several times the possibility of searching for that footage.

He found on the internet the name of one of the British reporters who had been sent to Rwanda by the B.B.C. between April and July 1994. He wrote him an e-mail.

I did not dare hope that we would get a reply.

A few days later, however, on December 6, one arrived.

Mark Doyle, "World Affairs Correspondent", wrote:

> *Dear Mr Mairesse,*
>
> *You ask a big question. I would like to be able to help, but I think I would need more detail. Then I could circulate your question around the half a dozen or so B.B.C. people who were present at the time of the genocide (as was I) and maybe it will jog their memory.*
>
> *I do have to warn you, though, that it is an extremely remote possibility that any film crew would have kept the "rushes" (unedited pictures) of such an event, and it is even [more] unlikely, even if this event went into an edited T.V. story, that we would keep the story – it may be somewhere in the archives, but it might be an almighty job finding it . . .*
>
> *We would need to know where exactly this took place – which border crossing with Burundi?*
>
> *When exactly?*
>
> *How do you know it was a B.B.C. crew? – were they black/white/Asian/male/female? How many of them? Did you or your wife speak to them? Were they with aid agency people or perhaps U.N.A.M.I.R. people? Do you know their names?*
>
> *I will do what I can to help – but please do not raise your hopes for the above reasons.*
>
> *Best wishes,*
> *(Signature)*

Although this response was full of caution, it gave birth to something new inside me. The beginning of a possibility. I started thinking of that image of us as a horizon. It became material, desirable.

The internet had become accessible to everyone in a way that it was not in 1994, and is now the repository of bountiful scattered archives, and an incredible meeting place where yesterday and today can enter into dialogue.

We promptly sent Mark Doyle the answers to his questions and waited, with our hearts in our mouths. I told him I remembered two young men, one fair-haired and one red-headed, who got into the truck with us. I told him the convoy took us from a secondary school in Butare to the border along the Akanyaru River, that once we had got there we had to get out of the truck, at which point a soldier had wanted to shoot my mother. It was the presence of the television camera that had stopped him.

After confirming that he was not part of the crew which accompanied the *Terre des Hommes* convoy, Doyle forwarded our message to his colleagues who were in Rwanda during the genocide.

Two days later, on December 9, 2007, we received this message:

> *I think there is a possibility that my colleagues Glenn Middleton, Tony Wende and I were on this convoy. We accompanied a* Terre des Hommes *convoy from the school to the border, although I am not sure of the date. But it is true that Glenn, who is the cameraman, is blond-haired, as is Tony, the sound recordist. Both were standing in the truck. I was driving directly behind them. My recollection is that the majority of the people on the convoy were young Tutsi escaping the genocide. We were stopped by Interahamwe several times on the road to the border.*[3]
>
> *Best wishes,*
> *Fergal Keane*

Thirteen years after the events, all it took was a few e-mails to find them again.

Mark Doyle, who was delighted, wrote to us:

> *I am just amazed that we have got this far in making such a tenuous connection. The world is really becoming smaller with this sort of communication possible!*

I realised the value of this chance, and from then onwards I totally invested myself in the enquiries my partner had initiated. From that point forward, I was the one who corresponded with everyone and who followed all the various leads. After thanking Fergal for his response, I explained that I was looking for the report in which people said they had seen us.

He answered without delay:

> *Dear Beata,*
>
> *It is quite extraordinary. Yes, we do have a film. But I would like to be sure that it was the correct evacuation we are talking about. It seems it almost certainly is. The convoy was accompanied by the* préfet *at the time, a Sylvain Nsabimana. In fact he is on trial at the I.C.T.R. at this present moment.*
>
> *I also remember that there was a Japanese aid worker on one of the trucks and a blonde woman as well as the man from* Terre des Hommes.
>
> *I remember that we went to the school first and filmed the loading of the children. My recollection is that most of those travelling were children. Some wore bandages because of their wounds. It was a very scary journey with the militia on the road.*
>
> *I am always haunted by the memory of Butare, especially the people who were outside the office of the* préfet. *They were Tutsi who had gone there to seek refuge.*

> *My telephone number is 0044 . . .*
> *If you could call me that would be very good.*

At the same time, another South African journalist from the B.B.C., who has also been sent to Rwanda in 1994 but not in the June crew, and been copied in to Doyle's message, answered from New Delhi:

> *I think that some of this footage could be with the International Tribunal at Arusha – please check with them.*

I did not follow this advice straight away. It would take me thirteen years and the progress of new technology enabling the creation of the online archives of the Tribunal for me to think about that lead again.

For the time being, in December 2007, I tried to reach Fergal Keane by telephone, without success. He contacted me again in January 2008 and we talked for a while about our memories of 1994. He told me he related the two weeks he spent reporting with his crew in a book, *Season of Blood, A Rwandan Journey*, published in 1995. He also said he was going to look for a copy of the documentary their crew made for the B.B.C.'s "Panorama" programme and that he would be able to give it to me if I came to London.

The year went by. Our son was born in the spring.

I contacted Fergal again in November 2008. Our child was old enough for us to be away from him for a few days, leaving him in the care of his paternal grandparents. Towards the end of my e-mail, which I have just recently reread, I wrote: "Now that I have become a mother, the question of the 'transmission of memory' and the possibility that I could show those images to my son, so that he understands how I survived, has taken on even more significance for me."

In his belated reply, Fergal apologised, saying that he had been unwell. At the time I did not know what his illness was and imagined that it was a simple winter flu.

We took the opportunity of a research conference to which my husband was invited to go to London in the following spring to meet Fergal. He asked to meet us at Waterloo station. He looked exhausted. He started by explaining that he had been hospitalised in a psychiatric unit and that his wife had some reservations about his coming to meet us. She was afraid that our meeting would revive the trauma of the genocide. He took us to a nearby restaurant to which he had also asked David Harrison to come. At 60 years old in 1994, David was one of the B.B.C.'s most respected producers. He was a former officer of the British army, and at the time of the genocide he happened to be the most experienced journalist and the best French-speaker. Fergal was only 33 at the time. Almost the same age as I was when I first met him in London.

I had brought with me a few photographs of me and my family before 1994, as if to prove that my story was true. Fergal and David did not remember me as one of the children in the group of evacuees. But our memories converged on several points. They had not noticed that their presence had saved my mother's life. I described the young soldier at the border who put his gun to her head, and the officer present, who prevented him from shooting by discreetly nodding at the journalists filming a few steps away from us.

The two men told us about their Rwandan journey. David described the Interahamwe militiamen at the border posts with an ironic euphemism: "They were very incorrect young men."

Fergal, visibly still haunted by what he had seen over there, lost his temper: "You mean they were bloodthirsty brutes, don't you?" They also told us about the other three members of the crew, all born on the continent. Tony and Glenn were White South Africans: the first was a journalist who was the sound recordist during the reporting, the second was the cameraman. They were joined by a third, for the sections that were filmed on the territory controlled by the genocidal Hutu: Rizwana (Rizu) Hamid, a British journalist of Pakistani origin who spoke fluent Swahili because she had grown up in Tanzania.

From what they told us that evening and from what I later read in Fergal's book, I was able to imagine what they lived through during those two weeks they spent in my country in June 1994.

When the genocide started, on April 7, Fergal and his colleagues were in South Africa, where they were preparing for the country's first multiracial elections. He recognised that he first paid little attention to the news from Kigali, as he was too busy reporting on the historic events unfolding in Johannesburg: "The world's attention was focused on the elections, and I had just spent four years preparing for that moment."

As a result of the election held from April 26 to 29, Nelson Mandela became president. The whole world was more interested in looking at that resilient and joyful Africa, which had put an end to the apartheid regime, rather than at the other, violent Africa of Rwanda, which was seen as "tribal".

It was therefore only at the beginning of June that the four journalists started reporting on the situation in Rwanda, entering the country from the Ugandan border, in other words from the side controlled by the Rwandan Patriotic Front,[4] which consisted mainly of Tutsi refugees whose families had fled the pogroms of the 1950s to the 1970s. The R.P.F. had been conducting guerilla warfare since the autumn of 1990 to force the Hutu powers to accept the return of the exiles. They had launched their attack from Uganda, where many of them were born or had grown up in refugee camps. Until 1994, the fighting in what was a civil war in all but name was concentrated in the north of Rwanda. A ceasefire had nevertheless been forged, accompanied by the deployment of a U.N. peacekeeping force. The negotiations conducted under the aegis of the "international community" had just been concluded with peace agreements that called for the sharing of power and the return of the refugees,[5] when the Hutu extremists, who rejected those peace agreements, set in train their plan to exterminate the Tutsi on April 7, 1994. From that day forward, numerous non-extremist Hutu ministers and politicians were also massacred, and an interim government composed of proponents of the "final solution" was installed.

The Inkotanyi rebels, as the soldiers of the R.P.F. were called, then took up arms again to seize power from the hands of the Hutu extremists.

David Harrison, the producer, had organised the B.B.C. reporting in advance, notably by contacting representatives of the R.P.F. based in Brussels, who had then informed the combatants on the front of the arrival of the team. The journalists were accompanied for a week by an R.P.F. officer in charge of information who had grown up in Uganda, who led them to the front where his camp was facing off a Hutu governmental army that was also occupied in committing massacres in collusion with the Interahamwe militia.

By the time their reporting began, more than half the country was already in the hands of the Tutsi rebels, who had discovered hundreds of execution sites on the hills they had liberated. One of these was at the church of Nyarubuye, where some 20,000 people were killed in mid-April. Fergal, David, Tony and Glenn were among the first foreign journalists to go there.

Fergal, the young reporter, writes at the start of the chapter he devotes to this macabre discovery: "How do I write this, how do I do justice to what awaits at the end of this road? As simply as possible. This is not a subject for fine words." He tells of the bodies strewn over the ground and whose decomposition had not yet erased the horror, the cries frozen on the faces, the smell like nothing known, impossible to take in, the rats. He talks of the journalists' suffocation, the whisky bottles and cigarettes they shared after they left the site and which barely allayed their stupor.

It was that scene in the church at Nyarubuye which continued to haunt the journalist when we met him in London in 2009.

Their reporting also led them to various zones of the country held by the R.P.F., notably where the fighting was raging around Kigali. When he said goodbye to the officer who had first escorted them, Fergal gave him a collection of Keats' poems, a book in which he had tried to find a measure of peace since setting foot in Rwanda.

The rest of their journey took place in the zone still held by the extremist Hutu government. The four men were met at the border with Burundi by Rizu Hamid, the young B.B.C. journalist who had already made several expeditions into that part of the country. Their new escort was a sergeant in the Rwandan government army. Rizu managed to convince him that it was in the armed forces' interests to authorise them to go to Butare, the southernmost city in the country, by explaining that the B.B.C. wished to have the "version of the other side".

In *Season of Blood*, Fergal Keane describes the various interviews he had with the Hutu dignitaries of Butare during the three days he spent in the city. The rector of the National University of Rwanda, a bilingual intellectual educated in Belgium and Canada, denied the massacres while sipping his whisky. He even invited Fergal, who is Irish, to watch television with his family, on the evening when Ireland was playing in the F.I.F.A. World Cup, which was taking place in the U.S.A. Fergal declined. He was unaware at the time that the rector's wife, Pauline Nyiramasuhuko, was the Minister for Family Welfare and the Advancement of Women in the interim government, and that she would soon make history as the first woman to be indicted for genocide. During their brief stay in Butare, the journalists also met the *préfet* Nsabimana (whose trial by the International Criminal Tribunal Fergal mentioned in his first e-mail in 2007). Nsabimana was appointed interim *préfet* in April 1994, the day after the assassination of his predecessor, who had been the only Tutsi *préfet* in the country. Nsabimana was put in that position by the leaders of the regime (including Pauline Nyiramasuhuko), the most extremist Hutu in a city that was considered too moderate for having delayed its participation in the genocide. Even though Nsabimana had until then been an official of no great note, he found himself de facto at the head of an organisation dedicated to the extermination of the Tutsi from the prefecture and would play an important role in facilitating the circulation of the *Terre des Hommes* convoys and therefore in our rescue. The B.B.C. journalist describes him in his book as an affable man, who was ready to supply them with a *laissez-passer* that would allow them to move around Butare. Nsabimana did not deny the killings in his prefecture but ascribed them to individual "hotheads" and to the war. He affirmed that the hundreds of frightened and starving Tutsi gathered in the grounds in front of his office were under his protection and not at any risk. Fergal Keane is on the mark when, in the documentary, he comments: "But I have the terrible feeling that, by the time this programme is broadcast, these people could be dead."

In order to show his good faith, the *préfet* informed the foreigners that he would try to help with the evacuation of several hundred orphans to Burundi the next day. A Swiss N.G.O. had assembled the children, some of whom were injured, others traumatised. He explained that he was in negotiations with the army to let them cross the border.

He showed himself willing for the B.B.C. team to cover this rescue operation and arranged to meet them the following day at the Karubanda social workers' training school where the N.G.O. was housing the children.

That is how our evacuation came to be filmed by the B.B.C. crew who accompanied us to the border. When we left for Burundi, the journalists and the *préfet* returned to Butare. Nsabimana was then stripped of his position.

Let's go back to that video from the B.B.C.

In April 2009, my husband and I left London with a promise from Fergal that he would send us the film he made in Rwanda. He had become one of the greatest voices of the B.B.C. and would easily be able to secure a copy of the "Panorama" programme from the archive services. He said he had not watched it again since 1994 in order not to revivify the trauma.

Weeks went by. I was impatient to receive the video. It was the same impatience I was to feel thirteen years later as I waited for the Italian photographer's files from *Terre des Hommes*. The people I contacted did not seem to realise the expectancy I felt each time a lead opened up perhaps to finding the missing picture at last. They had their own lives, their own problems and other priorities. How was it that they didn't seem to grasp my impatience, when they were on the ground at the time, and they knew what we went through? But maybe I was asking too much. Had other survivors, had the deportees, felt the same way when they looked for their own traces? Does the experience of genocide distort our sense of time compared to others'?

Eventually Fergal wrote to say that the film would be arriving soon. In his e-mail he also wrote:

Chère Beata,
[...] I want you to know that meeting you was one of the most important moments I have experienced since 1994. It's funny how the year 94 seems to be the end and the

beginning of things, it stands up like a tombstone and a signpost at the same time.

You see, I have carried feelings of guilt and helplessness since then, and I have been troubled badly by dreams and flashbacks. It is much better now, but the most important thing was to hear from you that we made a difference in the case of your life and that of your mother.

That is why I was overcome with emotion at the table. I guess there is still a lot of pain trapped inside. Rwanda is always there. Always.

But to see you and your wonderful husband, to see you guys happy and know that you have a beautiful child, well, that makes a big difference. Life must win. It simply must. And life can be very beautiful.

Thank you for the gift of hope, my dear Beata.

With love and my best wishes,

Fergal

The film arrived at last. I watched it three times back to back. I found in it much of what I had read in Fergal's book. And just as in the book, the part about the convoy of June 18 occupies a significant portion of the whole. You can see the children climbing into the trucks in the school yard in Butare, under the supervision of the humanitarian aid workers and the *préfet*. Then the road is filmed from one of the vehicles, the roadblocks where the militiamen armed with killing tools, machetes, scythes and clubs look at their little preys escaping them, with the *préfet* in his black sedan opening the way. He is interviewed at the border post. Wearing a fine, brightly coloured shirt, he explains with a smile: "In time of war, there are always children without fathers and mothers. I feel obliged to intervene and save them, no matter who they are. The child is who he is, the child is not responsible for the conflict or the problems of the country."

The sequence with the convoy finishes with a close-up of the *préfet* and the Swiss humanitarian worker from *Terre des Hommes* (whose name I did not know when I first watched it), leaning against the barrier at the border as they watch the children walking away. A second shot shows the children in the distance, a close-knit crowd advancing across the border towards the flag of Burundi.

I pushed "pause" several times and scrutinised the images, looking for my face and my mother's. But there was nothing. We did not appear in that documentary. Had we stayed out of the camera's field? Had the people who said they saw us on the B.B.C. lied? Or did they get it wrong? Unless "we saw you" meant the whole group of the convoy? I no longer have a precise memory of the time and the terms in which this information was given to us. And my mother's memory was even more riddled with holes than mine.

I assumed other images besides the ones shown in the "Panorama" programme were filmed that day, and that they had been broadcast in a television news bulletin. I would have to find the copies of the evening news of June 19 and 20, 1994. Were they preserved in the archives in London?

I asked. I got a reply saying there was nothing else.
That was all.

Bordeaux and Johannesburg, summer 2011

My husband received an e-mail from Tony (Hamilton) Wende, the sound recordist from the B.B.C. crew. In it he said he had written to us after the first joint e-mail Mark Doyle had sent us in 2007, but we had never received his e-mail. "I have photographs of the children in the trucks and these may interest you," he wrote. Wende explained that he had started giving journalism classes and that it was his students in a school in Lesotho, to whom he had told the story of the convoy, shown the photographs and mentioned my husband's e-mail, who had urged him to contact us again.

I opened the attachments with my heart pounding, hoping to recognise myself in one of the snapshots. I looked for my face in vain. I recognised the truck; that was the one we were in. I looked into the back of its huge container. My mother and I were not supposed to be there; according to the evacuation authorisation granted to the N.G.O. we were too old. So we had to be hidden, lying down in the bottom of the container, covered in pieces of fabric. That is how we travelled most of the time. When the truck was moving, with its doors half closed, we could sit up in the darkness and lift up a corner of the fabric to get some air. The children were aware of our presence, they knew they had to hide us from the killers looking into the dark container at the stops. Before each roadblock, where the militiamen opened the doors to look inside, we would lie down again under the fabric, motionless, holding our breath, and the little children at the back sat on top of us.

FOUR PHOTOGRAPHS

*

Tony sent four photographs. The first three show children sitting in a container truck. The fourth is an outdoor scene, taken at the barrier on the border. The photographs were numbered 56 to 60. Number 59 was missing.

The first one, number 56, is a view of the truck, a low-angle shot of the container with dark red panels and the two rear doors open, in which around fifty children are seated one on top of each other. They do not appear to be afraid. I imagine that the photographer took the shot standing on the back step of the truck. A few children stare into the lens, their faces unreadable, their heads slightly raised. The others, the vast majority of them, have their eyes turned towards something, or rather someone, who must be standing behind the truck, to the left of the photographer. Several children have a slight smile as they look at him. Some children are squatting, the smallest ones are sitting in the bigger ones' laps.

The second photograph, number 57, was taken facing the truck, almost looking down on it; all you can see is the first row of seated children, on the right-hand side. Their faces are more closed, without hostility but with serious expressions that are unusual for their age. I wonder if this photograph might have been the first one taken by the photographer and was later filed out of order. On the chests of several children, you can see white paper labels bearing their name and a number.

Photograph number 58 is a close-up, also taken from the back step. It focuses on the left flank of the truck. By comparing the patterns and the colours of the fabric of the children's clothing, as well as their faces, I can see there are some who appear on one or another of the two preceding photographs.

*

It is clear that the children were washed and dressed in nice clean clothes before getting into the truck. There is a disconnect between their appearance and the reality of what was happening. The Tutsi, hunted down in all the surrounding hills, had been in flight for more than two months, with unkempt hair and no opportunity to wash. Only the bandages on the children's bodies, the traces of the blows that they had survived, and their being crowded into this container usually reserved for sacks of merchandise or crates of beverages contradict the light-hearted, well-groomed appearance the photograph gives to them.

Number 60, taken later, shows around fifteen children standing up, leaning against the arm barrier marking the border between Rwanda and Burundi.

The barrier is painted red and white. On the slightly rusty counterweight on the left of the picture, there is a word written in chalk, in capital letters: "ARIYERI". I do not know what it means, but it is very probably the French word *arrière* (back) pronounced as the Rwandans do and transcribed phonetically. Unless it is a *barrière* (barrier), which has lost its "b". It is hot, there are a few pullovers hanging over the bars, and some are knotted around hips.

These children must have come mostly from the other truck for none of the faces are recognisable from the other photographs. They are looking at the photographer, who is on the Burundi side, as are two of the children in fact. It seems that the passage into the other country, imminent for some of the children, has already occurred for the youngest ones, who probably do not have the same notion of the physical materiality of a border. You can read the exhaustion on their faces; the journey is not yet over. In the older children's eyes, you can also see some anxiety. They have not yet made it across. They have no idea what will happen next, once they get to the other side. The memory of the killings that several of them only narrowly survived is still fresh. In the background you can make out the border post, a simple, elongated brick building under a tin roof with an extending eave that creates a shallow overhang where people in normal times could shelter from the sun or the rain. Further in the distance is a hillside with a few houses surrounded by banana trees. Were it not for the expressions on the faces of some of the children, who look like old men, you could almost believe this was a departure for a field trip or a holiday. A large family, brothers and sisters and cousins, all dressed in their best clothes, waiting patiently for their parents or group leaders to finish getting their passports stamped so they can cross the border.

When I received Tony Wende's e-mail, I first thought this was a new setback. Then I looked at photograph number 56 a little more closely. There is a shape there that only I can find meaning in, because I know its story. As crazy as this may seem, this photograph, on which my mother and I are not visible, is the proof that we really were hiding there. You can just make out a dark shape in the back on the right. I even think you can see a bit of my mother's afro hair. There is something in that corner that is full and empty at the same time, especially if you compare it to its opposite corner on the left, where the children are sitting all the way back, leaning against the end panel. This presence-absence tells the conditions of our survival, one roadblock after another, better than anything. I told myself that, for now, this trace was enough for me.

I thanked Tony and filed the photographs.
    I didn't spend any time on the other children. My quest at the time was purely personal, individualistic.

The other girls saved by *Terre des Hommes* whom I knew, such as my friend Annick and her sister Aline, were all part of the last convoy, the one in July. I could not imagine that they would be interested in the photographs of the June one.

The years passed, filled with reading that changed my attitude to documentary evidence, to archives.

Tourtour, summer 2022

When I took an interest in the photographs of the convoy again more than a decade later, what struck me was that there were four of them. That number reminded me of four other photographs, taken at Auschwitz-Birkenau, by the members of the *Sonderkommando*. As far as I know, these are the only images taken out of the extermination camp, besides those produced by the German executioners. The prisoners in the *Sonderkommando* were forced to evacuate the bodies and clean the gas chambers and cremation ovens. They were condemned to be murdered themselves: the teams were regularly changed, and the first task of each was the cremation of its predecessors.

It was in August 1944 that a group managed to get hold of a camera and take photographs. The film was hidden in a toothpaste tube and taken out of the camp by a Polish woman who worked there. She then gave it to Resistance activists in order to alert the Allies to the exterminations taking place in Auschwitz-Birkenau.

One can imagine the terrifying risks taken by the photographer to snatch those images from under the surveillance of the *Kapos*. He must have taken them furtively, from a distance, in the shortest possible time. The photographs have come to us numbered, by whom I do not know.

The first one, number 280, shows members of the *Sonderkommando* as they are burning bodies in a huge pit from which smoke is rising. The next one, number 281, shows the same scene but with two men who seem to be carrying bodies to throw into the fire.

The two following photographs are taken from another angle and with even more random framing. On the one numbered 282, you can see naked women heading towards a place which must be the crematorium. Behind them, a blurry group of people can be seen getting undressed under the barked orders of the *Kapos*.

As for the last photograph, it shows only trees in the sky, indicating that the photographer must have acted hastily and not been able to frame it properly. All that can be seen is a section of the birch forest surrounding Auschwitz-Birkenau.

Why did I think of these photographs specifically when I reconsidered those of my Rwandan convoy? Apart from their number, four, and the genocidal context, there was nothing to connect them. Those from 1944 tell the story of an extermination and were stolen from the concentration camp machine; they are the evidence of the worst, whereas the pictures taken at the Rwandan border 50 years later were taken freely, in the sight and knowledge of everyone present. They are part of a long series of images captured that day by still or film cameras belonging to journalists, to foreigners who were not threatened with death like the prisoners in the *Sonderkommando*. And above all, they are evidence of an escape towards life and not of an execution.

As I unravelled those arguments, I thought back to all the times I had tried to draw a parallel between the Holocaust and the genocide against the Tutsi and had noticed reactions of incomprehension or rejection in my interlocutors. I was aware fairly early on of the notion of the uniqueness of the Holocaust, but like many other Tutsi survivors, I believe, I kept reaching out to that story which took place half a century before ours, the one that has been the subject of the most important work on memory of these last thirty years, in both academic and creative fields.

FOUR PHOTOGRAPHS

When I arrived in France, I had the mistaken impression that the genocide of the Jews had always been a central element of European collective memory. There was something reassuring to me in identifying with that history: it was like a reference point that would allow me to express my grief to the rest of the world. I started journeying through the words of Imre Kertész, Primo Levi and also, later, Anna Langfus. For it seemed to me that their writing clothed my experience in an indispensable intelligibility.

In the middle of the 1990s, that history was very present in the public space in France. It was in 1995 that President Jacques Chirac gave his famous speech about the round-up of French Jews at the Vel d'Hiv, and it was from the autumn of 1997 to the spring of 1998 that the trial of Nazi collaborator Maurice Papon took place. I followed all that with great interest.

It was only much later that I understood the extent of the silence about the Holocaust in the first decades after the war. At the time, France needed to be reconstructed, its Resistance fighters glorified, and a national history forged in which the dehumanisation experienced in the camps had no place.

Two years ago, I was astounded to read the following statement in a memoir written in 1945 by Marguerite Duras, who had just welcomed home her husband Robert Anselme, a Resistance fighter who had returned from imprisonment in Germany in critical, skeletal condition: "De Gaulle doesn't talk about the concentration camps, it's blatant the way he doesn't talk about them, the way he is clearly reluctant to credit the people's suffering with a share in the victory."

If de Gaulle did not even speak about the concentration camps, and would support the nomination of Maurice Papon as treasurer of the U.D.R. political party a few years later, what could there be to say about the extermination camps and about all those people who had been killed when they were not "even" Resistance fighters, about those who were subjected to genocide solely for being Roma or Jewish?

I came to realise that the Jewish survivors had lived through decades of bitterness and silencing after the war.

I also became aware that what was presented as the "silence of survivors" actually masked a general refusal to hear their stories. French historian Annette Wieviorka explains it in this way, in a text published barely ten years ago: "researching the first testimonies of the deportation [of Jews from France], those written immediately after their return, [I had] been surprised by their number. Some of these accounts had been published by large publishing houses, others were self-published. It was said (and is sometimes still heard) that the deportees had not spoken. Their experience in the camps was, by all accounts, unspeakable, indescribable. In reality, it had been mostly inaudible." I read the memoirs and novels by Holocaust survivors with the keenness of someone hoping to benefit from the experience of their elders, hoping to recognise myself in them.

It sometimes happened that the identification I sought was denied to me.

I remember a time when I was invited to speak, alongside a gentleman who was a Holocaust survivor, having been a Jewish child hidden during the war, and how in my naive fashion I would say "we" in order to connect our destinies as survivors. Until he explained to me: "I do not know very much about what happened in your country, but it's true that Africa is in a sorry state, all those wars, all those coups, and then the poverty . . ." I looked at him in consternation, realising that, for him, what I had lived through was only what he saw as one of the countless troubles endured by the vast country-continent, the heart of darkness, where, as some people saw it, "people had been killing each other since the dawn of time". When I asked him whether or not he considered the particular events in Rwanda to be a genocide, he was silent for a while, then changed the subject.

Thankfully, during my journey, most of the survivors or children of survivors I met reached out to me, and I later found the assurance of recognition by the *Mémorial de la Shoah*, the Holocaust museum in Paris, which in recent years has hosted several events about the genocide against the Tutsi.

To get back to the four photographs, it was in *Bark*, the book by Georges Didi-Huberman, which I read during my writing residency at the *Fondation des Treilles* in Tourtour, that I found the most fitting words to articulate my feelings: "[. . .] not all images remain without shared consequences. Some images – like those of the *Sonderkommando* of Birkenau – are collective acts, not simple trophies or private trinkets."

Even if the four snapshots from 1994 were not simply the result of the incredible courage of a small group of condemned men, I had the sense, as I decided to set out in search of their protagonists, that they also carried the seed of some of that shared significance.

I could no longer keep them, private and useless, in a file on my computer. I needed to let them find their destiny one way or another, and to allow them to tell a collective story, one much greater than mine, of which I would be only the catalyst.

It is a story that I could not help but compare to that of the *Kindertransport*, those other convoys to life that enabled the transfer of thousands of Jewish refugee children from Germany, Austria, Poland and the Czech territories towards Great Britain between 1938 and 1940.

I first learned about these rescue operations in W.G. Sebald's novel *Austerlitz*. I then discovered, thanks to news reports and documentaries online, how nine to ten thousand children, including 7,500 Jewish children aged under seventeen, fled their country, most often by train or boat, alone, to escape the Nazis. On their arrival they were hosted by Jewish, Quaker or Christian families of volunteers, or, for the older ones, put up in youth hostels or on farms.

After the war, the children, most of whom had become orphans, their parents having died in the Holocaust, took on British nationality, or emigrated to other English-speaking countries or to Israel.

In 2009, a special train made up of a locomotive and wagons dating from the 1930s was chartered by the survivors and their children to make the journey symbolically again. On their arrival in England, they paid a moving homage to Nicholas Winton, one of the principal organisers of the *Kindertransport*, dubbed the "British Schindler".

Winton was a genuinely righteous individual who had said nothing about his good deeds for fifty years, until quite by chance his wife found among his things a satchel containing a list of the children and letters from their parents.

On discovering this story, I thought about the humanitarian aid worker who organised our Rwandan convoys, who had died before we were able collectively to thank him, and whose friends and neighbours were mostly unaware of what he had done for us. I thought about that list of names for which I had been searching for so many years. Was it sleeping in a forgotten folder in an attic somewhere or an archive box in Switzerland or Italy?

I continue to ask myself questions about my attempts to link our experience to the Holocaust. Was it because I had developed a special relationship to reading in childhood that books were the place I went looking for the meaning of my adolescent experience? To begin with, I only had books about the genocide of the Jews at my disposal. The films by Rithy Panh on the genocide perpetrated by the Khmer Rouge in Cambodia and the research into the Armenian and Roma genocides came much later.

Books have always been there for me, even before the genocide, like a refuge for the child that I was, who was always too different, with my working-class background and mixed race, considered White by Black people and Black by White people. I would read to escape the gloom of my daily life as a single child, when I was sometimes isolated because I was poorer than my classmates and fatherless. But rather than seeking out happy stories to escape my condition, I would latch on to destinies that were darker even than my own.

During the first weeks of the genocide, when my mother and I were living in seclusion in our apartment like silent and terrorised shadows, I would make the most of the daylight to read or reread continuously anything that I could find in our tiny book collection. The previous year, at the end of middle school, I had received a book about the history of the twentieth century, presented by the international school of Butare. That private institution was attended mostly by the children of expatriates or of the wealthiest Rwandans and was connected to the Belgian educational system; I was only able to enrol because of an external sponsorship arrangement. That is where I learned to read and write in French as a very young child, and where I had acquired a knowledge of the Western world that would be helpful in allowing me to adapt very quickly to life in France on my arrival. But at the time, in April 1994, when most of my old schoolmates had already been evacuated, I was still there, reading that history book alone, paying particular attention to the pages about wars. Then I read an old paperback book that had never attracted me before – I still have no idea how it happened to be in our apartment – the first volume of *War and Peace*. No doubt the title seemed relevant to me. I never tried to read the second volume once I got to France. Another item of my reading at the very beginning of the spring of 1994 made a lasting impression on me: *I Am Fifteen – And I Do not Want to Die*, by Christine Arnothy. I made a reference to it in the short diary I kept during that first period in hiding, before my mother slid it underneath the heavy wardrobe in her bedroom, and – ironically – we went to hide in a cellar, just like the book's narrator.

Nearly thirty years later, as I write these memories, I can see that the peculiar teenager I was at the time must have lived through the beginning of the genocide in a mixture of lucidity and maturity, but also in a kind of novelistic hallucinatory state, in which my life blended with those of the heroes of my reading, and which would soon be swept away by brute fear in the face of permanent danger.

Books have always been there for me. Photographs too.

When we had to leave our apartment precipitously to go to our first hiding place in April 1994, I had tucked my photograph album into the little blue Speedo sports bag with which I would cross the border two months later.

The album contained mostly scenes from the international school, snapshots given to me by European parents or teachers, who took lots of them because they had cameras. School celebrations, themed meals, fêtes and birthdays. And then a few family photographs.

Unlike the expats, few Rwandans owned a camera. In Butare, people used to go to the photographer in the Arab neighbourhood to have their portraits taken in front of a plaid curtain or a painted backdrop, artless scenes that could be found in the albums of an entire generation. Sometimes, when financial resources allowed, a photographer would be hired to come to the house to immortalise a particular event – a baptism, a wedding – or because the children were growing up and it seemed important to keep a record of their life.

No doubt like people all over the world, Rwandans loved to give or send each other their photographs, in which they often stood fixed in identical poses, in front of a pot plant, a bouquet of flowers or a shrub, looking respectable and serious.

When people went to visit friends, the conversation invariably turned to family or common acquaintances, and always ended with someone getting out the album and everybody contemplating and commenting at length on the faces stashed away between the cardboard pages covered in plastic film that had yellowed with time.

Then a spiralling conversation would start, in which all the genealogies would intersect and the clans of each person were listed. Now I think about it, it seems there was never any discussion of the "ethnicity" of a person, which perfectly illustrates the fact that traditionally it was the *ubwoko* (which the colonial powers translated as "clan", although the word means the eighteen large community groups, each of which brings together the descendants of a single ancestor) that was more important than "ethnicity". Later, I would learn that in Rwandan cosmology, the Tutsi, the Twa and the Hutu shared the same ancestors, and that this idea of ethnicity was a racist interpretation inherited from the colonial period. While the Hutu and Tutsi groups had in fact always existed, and the former were the crop growers and the latter the pastoral farmers, they did have a language in common, the same culture, and the same religion, and lived together on all of the national territory of Rwanda, which had been a kingdom since the fifteenth century.

The portraits that we looked at in the family albums did not bear captions indicating the person's ethnicity, unlike the identity cards imposed in the beginning of the 1930s by the Belgian occupiers, I.D. cards that would be systematically checked by the militiamen at the roadblocks during the genocide. We could talk for hours about the long and colourful history that linked Hilaria or Jeanne, posing demurely on page 1, with the uncle of the godmother of Radegonda, whose black and white portrait, with bell-bottom trousers and afro hairstyle, was at the bottom of page 10. The connections were so numerous – those who had studied or worked together, the marriages, the friendships, the neighbours – that those afternoons spent leafing through the albums perfectly illustrated this reality: that Rwanda was a tiny country where everyone knew everyone else. And everyone knew what was written on everyone else's identity card, even if it was never mentioned in conversation.

After the genocide, because few people had the presence of mind or the possibility of taking their photograph albums with them or of putting them in a safe place, and because the killers systematically destroyed all traces of the Tutsi, even those on glossy paper, a desperate chain of correspondence was started between survivors or relatives living abroad to try to find a few images of those whose lives were lost.

Photographs were important. They are still important, especially those of the deceased. At the Gisozi genocide memorial, in Kigali, there is a small room with its walls covered in their photographs, clipped onto fine metal cables under dimmed lights. They tell of the shimmering life before the disaster. When the month of April comes around each year, survivors post pictures of their dead on the "walls" of their social networks. In Rwanda lots of people have slightly kitsch frames in their living rooms with collages made up of a few preserved photographs. Those pictures are material evidence for them, a fragile bulwark against the frittering of memory.

2

The Tense of Testimony

"For all of us, this is still a miracle we cannot fathom."
Convoy to Auschwitz: Women of the French Resistance
Charlotte Delbo
Translated by Carol Cosman

I have just celebrated my fifteenth birthday.
I live with my mother in Butare, the second city in Rwanda, in the south, not far from the border with Burundi.

* * *

This is my story as it came to me, spontaneously, a few days ago, in front of the students of the *Lycée Thierry Maulnier* in Nice. I am telling the events of the past in the present. For me, the tense of testimony can only be the present, since relating those instants is an exercise that brings them back to life with particular force. It allows the adolescent of yesterday to stand before the woman in her forties today and to abolish the distance between then and now.

When the necessity of writing about the convoys organised by *Terre des Hommes* became clear to me in 2020, I had not planned to tell my own personal experience of the genocide. And then two years later, at the midpoint of my writing residency where I had gone to write the story of the convoy of June 18, I received an invitation from Bénédicte Gilardi and Muriel Blanc, respectively the teacher-librarian and social studies teacher of the *Lycée Thierry Maulnier* (now *Lycée Mélinée et Missak Manouchian*), to come to speak to their senior students. I had been there each year from 2016 to 2019. It was during that last visit to Nice that I had met Rodrigue. It was there that this whole quest to find the children of the convoy had begun. Life is made up of intersecting rings, of loops of troubling serendipity.

When I got home from the encounter with the school students in Nice in 2022, it seemed obvious to me that I could not avoid telling the story of my survival in this book, the story of the two and a half months from the start of the genocide on April 7 to June 18. I could not write about the convoys without giving an account of my own intimate experience of the genocide, although that was something I had always guarded against until then, preferring to invent fictional characters who were close but not identical to me. It became clear I needed to commit to writing in a book what had, until then, been entrusted to the loose and ephemeral fabric of speech.

I am setting down these words as they came to me in front of those students. I will try to provide an unadorned account, although I am aware that it may be polished out of newly formed habit, by my writer's language.

The schoolteachers had told their students: "Beata is not going to tell you her personal history, she never does; she is going to talk about her experience as a survivor who writes fiction, about her relationship with literature." That is what I had restricted myself to on the previous occasions.

But since then, I had accepted to talk about my memories, first in fragments then giving a little more each time, in front of school groups at the Shoah Memorial in Paris, then in a *lycée* in Brussels, then another one in Castres.

In 2021, I had talked a lot about the *Terre des Hommes* convoy during a literary festival at the Jan Michalski Foundation, no doubt because I was in Switzerland, the country that the humanitarian aid workers who had saved me had come from. Then a short time later, at the Shoah Memorial again, where a presentation about rescue operations during genocide had been organised in partnership with the Ibuka France charity.

I was compelled to leave behind the comfort of fiction and to accept the role, so necessary yet so heavy, of a naked witness.

So here is what I ended up telling the *lycée* students in Nice, motivated as I was by this new urge to tell my story.

I have no brothers or sisters and Maman is a single mother. So there are just the two of us when everything starts.

I have an uncle on my mother's side who lives with his wife and three of their five children out in the countryside, on the hill where my mother comes from. His oldest daughter, my cousin Rafiki, goes to a secondary school in Butare, and has just come home for the Easter holidays. Laurent, the oldest of my cousins, had been visiting our family exiled in Tanzania when the civil war broke out in 1990. We have not seen him since, but we found out that he had joined the R.P.F. army, the exiled Tutsi who want to return home. In April 1994 we do not know whether he is alive or dead.

Butare is a university town with many intellectuals and students, and the only city in the country with a Tutsi préfet, just recently appointed. This says something about how little importance is given in our prefecture to the extremist ideology furthered by the Hutu from the north who hold the reins of power, which has become more virulent since 1990.

The genocide starts on April 7 in Kigali then quickly spreads to the remaining prefectures of the country, but the killings only break out in Butare on April 20.

The genocidal authorities from the north (the area where President Habyarimana came from, and whose assassination served as the pretext for the start of the genocide although it had been prepared long beforehand) want to be assured that the inhabitants of Butare will not evade participation in the extermination operation. And so they appoint several people from our city to the government, as well as the acting president of the republic, who will ensure the massacres are carried out, notably the Prime Minister and the Minister for Family Affairs and the Advancement of Women.

The first few days, we hear disturbing news about massacres in Kigali. We learn from a few people who were able to leave the capital and find refuge in the south that such and such a family has been exterminated. Things are still uncertain, we hope that "this" will not come as far as our city.

But the accounts of massacres are getting closer. A general curfew has been declared, the shops are shut, food reserves are quickly dwindling. On April 10, because a soldier entered the hotel complex near where we are living and threatened to set off a grenade, we ask for shelter with some friends of ours who are nuns. The one who is closest to my mother, Christine, a French nun whose family have been sponsoring me for a few years, is in France at the time. It is her colleague, a Canadian nun, who takes us in. She tells us we can spend the night in one of the houses belonging to the order that sit in the grounds of the secondary school the sisters are in charge of, but that we will need to leave very early the next day.

Our return home that morning is distressing. We are more terrorised than ever after walking up the main street of Butare which is completely deserted. We do not have much food left at home, we have no other place to go.

THE CONVOY

There are already rumours that the killings of Tutsi have started in the surrounding hills.

We barricade ourselves into our little apartment, which is in the annex of an old hotel complex, with an entrance that is not easily visible from the main street, because it is in the recess of a wall with nothing facing it. Few people know there are living quarters there, and that probably protects us for a while.

However, one day, a hand discreetly scratches at our door. Through the fine mesh, we can see that the tall thin man standing there is as frightened as we are. And so we open up. He says he has fled from a country town north of Butare. His clothes are torn. He clearly has not washed or slept in a bed for several days. He speaks little, seems afraid of frightening us if he were to describe what he saw back there. He is hungry. We offer him some boiled red beans that are starting to taste rancid and our last spoonful of rice.

In one breath, he says: "I have to keep going. You can't stay here either. You should find somewhere to hide." He has no idea where he will go, but his only option seems to be to keep moving.

I will never forget the look in his eyes, like a hunted animal, or his hands that never stopped shaking while he was eating.

But where can we go?

A few days earlier, all the foreigners left the city, escorted by Belgian para-commandos who came to Rwanda expressly to evacuate them. I often think of the long line of cars in the main street, filled with suitcases, ready to leave. Butare is like a village, and because I went to the international school, we know everyone. Most of the people avoid making eye contact with us. They must know or sense that we will be killed. They are afraid that we will ask them for help.

* * *

When I talk to the school class about that moment, I feel a furious urge to burst into tears. A mixture of resentment and stupefaction that has never left me. But I brush those feelings away, because I cannot let myself be devoured by bitterness.

What would I have done in their place? Probably the same thing.

* * *

My mother suggests putting me in the care of one of the families or of the nuns, begging them to save at least my young life. 'They can't refuse, you are mixed race, they will let you over the border with no problems.'

I am the one who refuses.

I tell my mother I do not want to leave her by herself. My decision seems to comfort her and annihilate her at the same time.

From that moment on, our roles start to be reversed. I can see that she is more and more helpless, that it is impossible for her to protect me, and that I will have to make decisions for both of us.

Where can we find refuge?

The proprietor of the hotel, and therefore also of the apartment that we rent, is Tutsi, the widow of a Hutu man. She too is therefore in danger. In these moments of distress, class barriers are no longer so important.

She confides in my mother that she is looking for a

way to escape to Burundi and promises to warn her when the time comes so that we can leave with her and her five children. Shortly afterwards, as I am looking out of the window from behind the sheer curtains, I see a vehicle go by. They are leaving without us, in secret. These are troubled times; how many people are willing to take risks for others?

We have lost all hope.

On Friday, April 22, all we have left to eat are a few withered potatoes. Someone knocks at our door again, with great assurance this time. It is a soldier, who is shouting: "Open up, I know there are people in here." We comply, resigned, trembling. He is not armed and does not appear threatening. He walks all around the apartment, with us on his heels. He must be looking for something of value, but we are not rich. His eyes fall on our bicycles. I got a beautiful pink bike for my thirteenth birthday, it is my most precious possession. And my mother recently bought a bottle-green Dutch bike from some Belgians who were going home after a few years working in Rwanda.

The soldier leaves, pushing a bicycle with each hand. He tells us, with unbearable lightness: "You're going to be killed soon anyway, so you won't need them."

Since the beginning of the genocide, we have been talking regularly with the hotel employees, some of whom will soon play an important role in our survival.

One of them is a cook, the other a waiter; they are Tutsi, but they have identity cards that present them as Hutu, which protects them. The cook managed to get his in his hometown, by bribing a clerk; as for the waiter, I *think he used a razor blade to scrape off the ballpoint line crossing out the word "Hutu" and crossed out "Tutsi" instead. What actually protects them most in the following three months is that they both come from the back-country hills and nobody knows their true identity in Butare. The waiter will survive, but I will learn much later that the cook was killed towards the end of June, when his true identity was finally unmasked. They will get occasional help from two Hutu colleagues, the gardener and his father who works as the night watchman, helpers whose attitude over time becomes increasingly uncertain.*

The soldier from Friday has gone and told everyone in town that the two magnificent bicycles were gifts (!) from Tutsi (of which one was a White girl) living in such and such a place. The hotel employees suggest we leave the apartment before other looters arrive.

The waiter hides us in one of the hotel rooms, which is empty at the time. It is room number 13, situated at the end of a long, one-storey building, in a discreet corner partly hidden by a tall plant.

Is it that plant that saves us, thanks to a gust of wind or the April diluvian rains, with its branches barring the door behind which we are hunched up?

The day after we move in there, the soldiers search all the empty rooms of the hotel. All except ours.

Officers from the capital have moved to Butare, requisitioning another part of the hotel. Are they occupying some of the rooms, or only the restaurant? My memories on this point are indistinct. What is certain is that their presence is a real threat. We are now in the middle of the hornets' nest.

I would think about this situation later, as I was reading Edgar Allan Poe's story, "The Purloined Letter", for my university preparatory studies in English. Perhaps it is precisely because we were in the very heart of one of the army headquarters that we were not found?

* * *

Our saviours of the moment then decide it is time we change hiding places. We have to go into a cellar.

The hotel, built in the period of Belgian colonisation, is one of the very few buildings in the country that has a basement. This is an architectural peculiarity that is completely unknown to most Rwandans. The risk that killers should find us there is close to nil.

Our transfer takes place at night. Thirty metres at most separate room number 13 from the kitchens where we will find the door down to the cellar. The city is plunged into darkness since power has been cut off for some time now. We have to make the most of the dark to get over there without being seen.

We follow the waiter once again, walking on tiptoe, as close as possible to his shadow, so as not to lose sight of him. It is a moonless night, but a storm is brewing.

* * *

"Life hangs only by a thread."

All those expressions people often use to talk about others, or about distant events, without really according them any importance, almost automatically, until the day comes when one of them describes exactly what you are going through. "Life hangs only by a thread." This time I am repeating that phrase to the young people listening to me in silence, attentively. They are imagining that moonless night. They are trying to figure out what that must have meant for the woman standing before them, when she was their age, back there, back then.

* * *

For a moment, the sky is lit up by lightning, then everything is plunged into darkness again. I have enough time to see a soldier standing in the courtyard smoking a cigarette. Right in front of us. Our guide sees him too. We were about to bump into him. From that moment on, we keep well away from the little glowing point of light that is the end of his cigarette, like a hazard beacon we have to steer around so as not to be discovered.

In all my short life, I have never set foot in a basement. I think my first surprise is physical: it's cold and damp in there. A kind of dampness I have never known, that my pores do not know how to respond to. There seems to be something icy running down the walls; there is also a strange, incessant rubbing noise.

A thin foam mattress has been laid out on the ground for us. Very soon it will become a kind of soft sponge filled with water. We try to sleep on it, but I think I am the only one who actually drops off. My mother, always on the alert, can barely close her eyes.

The second shock takes place the next morning. It is daytime, and that is when I understand that we are in the belly of the earth. A small dirty skylight above our heads connects with the kitchen storage room and lets a little light filter through. My eyes follow that yellow thread across the walls. They are covered in bugs, which I can't quite make out, just that they are dark and moving. It is only when the cook brings us something to eat, holding a little paraffin candle, that I can identify them: they are cockroaches, as big as thumbs, hundreds of them.

* * *

At that point in my story, I explain to the children the irony of this colony of cockroaches that was sheltering us in our escape. I tell them about the hate speech of the extremist propaganda, used to dehumanise the Tutsi, calling them cockroaches, *inyenzi*, or snakes. And I add, just to lighten the atmosphere, for that is necessary sometimes: "So we are cockroaches hiding among other cockroaches."

* * *

How many days do we stay in that basement? One of the Tutsi employees at the hotel, one of those who were being hidden by their colleagues, comes to join us. For the duration of the genocide, we will share our hiding place for a few days at a time with a succession of people we will not see again, some of whom will not survive.

* * *

Sometimes I feel bad that I do not remember their names, or only part of them: there was Joseph and Gilbert, that much I know for sure, but what was the name of the one we nicknamed Kajisho, because of his damaged eye? Bosco or Safari? The names Muyibi and Karenzi also seem to come from that time. And the lady that was hiding with us at the end, was her name Consolata, or is that just my memory playing tricks on me? I regret not having remembered what all of them said to us in the thick of the anxiety that kept us awake, on high alert, even when the killers were asleep. In a little black notebook that I kept as a precious memento, I jotted down, at the very end of the 1990s, a few dates, a few names, so I would not forget them, promising myself that I would fill in the gaps later, before time eroded too much of my memory. But life and its imperatives got in the way of that project. I took it up twenty years later only to discover the extent of the loss.

* * *

The place is so damp that the candle we use once a day to see what we are eating goes out almost as soon as it is lit. And then sometimes my hand, trying to pick up a piece of sweet potato from the communal dish, picks up a huge cockroach instead.

After a few days, I start having breathing problems. Karoli, the cook, finds a Ventolin inhaler somewhere, but it does no good, I have to leave this place. We resign ourselves to going back up to the surface, where the risk of being found is much greater.

The hotel complex offers other hiding places. During colonial times, there was a theatre in the building, later transformed into a cinema, which was operational until the 1980s. The vast room now serves as a warehouse for a wealthy shopkeeper, Mwami, for whatever goods he needs to store. In the spring of 1994, it is truck tyres, piled up into strange black rubber towers. The hotel seems to be spared from looting. The people hiding us say that this is thanks to the chief of the military camp in Butare, who is a friend of the proprietor.

We go back through our old apartment, which has a

secret doorway into the old cinema. We spend a few days in that surrealist setting. The magician cook Karoli manages to bring us a daily plate of food, not much, but enough to survive on. The hotel has a large vegetable garden that allows us not to starve, and Karoli invents a thousand tricks to get into our present hiding place without being seen by the soldiers.

One of his other Tutsi colleagues has joined us in the old cinema and we go through all sorts of scenarios with our new companion in misfortune, imagining that if the killers arrived we would each slip into the middle of one of the towers of piled-up tyres by going through the stage of the old theatre.

The room we are in has a window looking out onto the main street; its glass has been covered by beige paint since it became a storage depot. I scratch a little circle in that paint, the size of a marble, and start keeping watch on the movements outside. The street is generally deserted. Sometimes an igitero goes by, the name given to the bands of killers that could be translated as "group of attackers". Then I pray that no-one sees my eye stuck to the windowpane, while also being incapable of keeping away from it. We take turns at this improvised observation post, where we sometimes gesture to the others: "Come and see this!" One afternoon, we see a young Hutu man go by, a schoolteacher we know. He is walking in slow motion, his face grave and showing a bushy beard. We would later find out that his wife, a Tutsi, had just been killed. The gardener and his father regularly return to their home hill, on the outskirts of the city. Every time they go there, they glean a little more information about *the massacres underway, which they share with the cook, who in turn passes it on to us.*

They are the ones who tell us about the first murder committed in the centre of Butare, the day after the visit of the interim president, whose speech was the starting gun of the genocide in our part of the country. We heard a gunshot. The bullet hit Karenzi, a Tutsi university professor we used to see riding past on his black bicycle. He was shot down just across from the hotel, in the little bamboo grove next to the university bookshop.

From that day onwards, there will be constant killings in Butare. From our various hiding places, we hear shouts and cries, sometimes dogs that the militia has trained to track down Tutsi hiding in the woods in the valley. We rarely hear gunshots. You have to pay money to be killed by a bullet rather than by a nail-studded club or a machete. And even when they pay, many people are deceived. We hear all these sounds and our imagination fills in the rest. Our food rations generally arrive with the obituaries: today it was so and so along with such and such who were hacked up.

My mum, who was already very thin, is getting more emaciated by the day. I try to close my ears and eat what I can.
I have decided to stay alive.

* * *

Sometimes I think it was my youth, my insolence in the face of death, that saved us. I was convinced that we would not die.

* * *

And yet not a day goes by without us learning about the death of someone we know. Karoli is in tears as he tells us how, according to what is being said in town, the militiamen killed the wife of my English teacher. She was pregnant. "They cut her belly open," he says, and his voice breaks as he adds: "They said she was expecting twins. Yebabaweee."

He is the one who explains that the killers, who were formerly farmhands, labourers or other workers, now say they are "going to work" when they go off to kill, and not just kill to get a job done, but torture, humiliate, martyrise their victims with a degree of macabre inventiveness that is just unbelievable. It was with the word "work" that they described the act of cutting open that woman. I think her name was Angélique.

* * *

And now I can't stop thinking that the word "work", which I can no longer pronounce lightly in our language, was also the one that the Nazis chose to use in Auschwitz to welcome the people they would soon exterminate. The sign above the entrance to the camp, which I visited in 2005, announced "*Arbeit macht frei*": work sets you free.

* * *

From our hiding place in the old theatre, I scan the street through the hole I scratched in the paint, hoping for I know not what. Most of the time, it is just so that I do not have to stay motionless waiting for a death which I refuse to accept will find us. One day a pickup truck bearing the United Nations logo stops in front of the grocery store across from the cinema.

* * *

I can't remember if the store was open at the time. How could it have been? Its owner was a Tutsi woman. So why was that vehicle there? It's a mystery.

* * *

I immediately signal my mother to show her this providential vehicle. We soon get very excited. If we could somehow manage to throw ourselves into that truck, without the militiamen posted at the roadblock further up the street seeing us, we would be saved. No-one would come and kill us under the noses of the Blue Helmets. How naive we are!

There's no time to grab a bag, we have to make a run for it, to get across the street. Now.

As my mother is opening the door to leave, something (once again, who knows how to account for these tiny miracles?) persuades me to check the spyhole one last time. I just have time to pull my mother back inside. The pickup truck must have been stolen from the United Nations forces. A soldier from the genocidal government army has just got out. We almost threw ourselves into the wolf's jaws.

* * *

I tell the students about another similar moment, when we were still in the basement.

* * *

My mum is at the end of her tether. She suddenly stands up, unsteady on her feet, and says, in a desperate, thin voice, that she is going to leave her hiding place and give herself up. With all the authority of my fifteen years, for the first and last time in my life, I slap her across the face. "You are going nowhere. We have to live."

* * *

It took my becoming a mother myself for me to understand what she went through during those months in hiding. Being unable to protect her child, knowing that at any moment her daughter could be killed before her eyes. Seeing her going hungry, being afraid, without having anything to give her. I developed particular phobias that I know come from that time. When I stopped breastfeeding my sons, an irrational question popped into my head: "What if we have to flee our home suddenly, and I do not have any more milk to feed them?" Each year when the month of April comes round, I always make a mental list of all the people I know, the neighbours or the acquaintances on whom we could count to hide us. If everything should start all over again. The strict injunction I give my children not to open the door to anyone before they have checked who is knocking. My eldest could not care less. "What do you think will happen to me?" I have explained it all to him, he understands that sometimes I can't help imagining it will be a man with a machete or a knife ready to kill them. He accepts my rules, but only to reassure me, for we have agreed that it is only my trauma, and not his.

The slap I gave my mother woke her up. I fear it may have rung out too loud in our silence populated with cockroaches, that its clacking sound reached the ears of the soldiers above our heads.

Maman sits back down on the mattress and never says anything again about giving herself up.

The days go by, slow and poisonous with constant anxiety. We listen to the news when we can on Mum's little transistor radio. Radio France Internationale and the Voice of America on the short-wave stations, whose news bulletins often talk about Rwanda.

Elsewhere on earth, life continues, placidly. Birthdays are celebrated, the winter draws back, spring warms everyone's hearts. There are preparations for the football World Cup in the U.S.A. On May 10, Nelson Mandela is elected president of the Republic of South Africa. The high dignitaries of the world come to Pretoria to attend his investiture. Africa is so happy with the end of apartheid.

On June 6 at Omaha Beach in Normandy, President Mitterand celebrates the fifty-year anniversary of the Allied landing. Journalists report his speech, in which – how ironic for someone we know supported the genocidal Rwandan government! – he says: "May the conflicts around us – in former Yugoslavia – and further from us – in Black Africa – and in countless other places in the world that only bring death be appeased! May dialogue be organised everywhere for peace between the nations and peoples of the world, under the auspices of our United Nations, which were born of our victory!"

We no longer expect our liberation from the Blue Helmets or the Western para-commandos. The only radio that gives us real hope is Muhabura, the voice of the Rwandan Patriotic Front (R.P.F.), the Tutsi rebels who have taken up arms again and will soon control the country. The transistor radio informs us of the fighting; the voice of the R.P.F. obviously mentions only their victories and advances. In some programmes, people who have just been delivered from their torture by the soldiers are interviewed. One day, we recognise a neighbour's children, who survived at their grandparents' house, where they had gone to spend the Easter holidays. They say that the militiamen gave them bread and Fanta, they say in their little childlike voices that they hope to find their mum and dad, who stayed in Butare. From this side of the war, we know that their parents have been killed.

* * *

I do not know why I remembered that story about bread and Fanta. Maybe because we were constantly hungry.

* * *

The cook does his best to give us a frugal daily meal with what the gardener brings him. Some days we have to make do with a few bananas.

* * *

Later on, when I hear other survivors talk about how they ate roots and drank muddy water, I realise, once again, how fortunate we were.

* * *

One day when he found me particularly sad, Karoli accomplished a miracle of goodness. With a carrot, a lettuce, an avocado, a few potatoes and especially a bottle of oil he fossicked out from who knows where, he prepares what I consider a feast for me. The lump of gratitude in my throat is so tight that my first bites are hesitant. It feels strange to get more emotional about a good meal than about how death is prowling all around me. Of the men who are hiding us, Karoli is the most generous and friendly. His family is on his home hill and he has no idea whether they are still alive or not. When he finds a toy or a book in the hotel, he brings it to me, a huge little present, a forlorn way of preserving some of my childhood. He must be hoping other people are doing the same thing for his four-year-old son.

* * *

Karoli was killed at the very end of the genocide in Butare. I found out about this much later. Who betrayed him?

At the beginning of the 2000s, when she was training as a social worker, my cousin Rafiki, who survived, found Karoli's son in an orphanage. She put me in contact with him. In my own way, I was able to show that child the gratitude I felt for his father's good deeds.

* * *

The last hiding place we occupy is another hotel room, number 1, which is more spacious than our first one, almost a studio. It is on the northern end of the hotel complex and a courtyard separates it from the proprietor's abandoned house. A woman in her forties, who was a friend of the proprietor, and was visiting when the genocide started, found herself alone in the house when the family left for Burundi. At least that's what I understand. This woman joins us in our new hiding place.

As for the four young Tutsi employees of the hotel, I believe they are in one or other of the two basements.

At the beginning of June, the hotel dogs howl every night.

We are attacked in broad daylight, on June 7. Late morning or early afternoon, I can't quite remember. Time doesn't flow normally when you have been in hiding for so long.

They arrive, overflowing with noise and hatred. A horde. First they drag the four young men from the basements. Two are killed on the spot, still dazzled by the glare of the sun outside. Two others manage to escape by running towards the vegetable plot then jumping over the wall into the little woodland in the valley. That is what we are told later.

We hear shouts. The killers are the ones yelling, not the victims. Fear liquefies us. The closed curtains of the room keep us in semi-darkness, motionless. The noise from outside comes to us with biting acuity. We can hear everything. We huddle together, Maman and I, sitting on the edge of a bed. The other woman has curled into a ball, on the floor, with her hands over her ears. We do not even try to crawl under the beds as we had done in room number 13 during the first search.

    I feel like I am melting, like an ice cube on the fire, and boiling at the same time. Thousands of little bubbles are popping in my head then seem to be flowing out of my ears to crash against the outside sounds, as onto rough granite boulders.

* * *

I have never felt that sensation, that fear, since then. But will the people who read these lines, will the children listening to me understand that word the same way as I do? As Mado, the companion in imprisonment of Charlotte Delbo, said so well, people use words lightly, unaware of what they mean for the survivors: "You hear them say, 'I almost fell, I got scared.' Do they even know what fear is?"

Decades later, one stormy day when I was watching the ocean throw itself at the stone flanks of the Atlantic coast, I saw a physical manifestation of what had been happening in my body on that day in the middle of June 1994, when I was about to die.

I am writing this testimony on a train taking me to a birthday party, at the other end of France, a few days after my presentation to the students in Nice.

I always need this kind of space to write the first few lines of my books. It's strange, this need to be part of an immobile crowd, in an impersonal space that is both in motion and contained, in order to dare to start on the most difficult writing: the first page or, in this case, the testimony that before today I have never yet dared to put down on paper.

When I was writing fiction about the genocide, I sometimes drew on historical events in order to make my descriptions more realistic. But then, if I felt overcome by emotion because I was exploring those still painful zones, I always had the option of seeking refuge again in my imagination, of creating an outcome that was less painful than what actually happened. In the same way, when I talk to students, my concern not to distress them or go over the allotted time serves as a welcome alibi not to say anything about certain events.

This ten-hour return journey leaves me no excuse. I am going to have to write this story, from end to end, with no detours. Why on a train? I come up with something of an answer, no doubt incomplete: perhaps because the movement of the carriage, or the landscape rushing past in my field of vision, reassures me about the fact that I am leaving. With this journey I can relive the hope I felt during that first important departure, the one in the convoy.

THE TENSE OF TESTIMONY

* * *

In this train taking me from Draguignan to Paris, I wonder whether, once I have written my testimony, I will be released from the spell, and be able to see that cursed month of June 1994 as a time like any other, one that existed of course, but that I have no need to return to. And will this mean that I won't have to go and talk to school groups until I am a very old lady, that I will be able to avoid the exhaustion I felt when I saw Evelyn Askolovitch speak to the *Lycée Thierry Maulnier* in Nice?

Were the people who published their accounts able to rest from speaking afterwards? The few times that I agreed to tell my story literally exhausted me. The following days, I needed a lot of sleep and to entrust my painful knotted back to the hands of physiotherapists and osteopaths.

Will I be able to replace this gruelling but necessary exercise with a recommendation to read my book?

Let's see.

June 7, 1994
I have no idea how many of them there are. A liquid terror is clouding my vision. It stops me from looking at them too long.

First, they break one of the windows into our room. We can see a stick lifting up the curtain that stopped them seeing inside. A face leans in to scan the room. No prayer can yet come to hang from our lips. Clasping each other, we slide down to the ground, curled up on the cement floor between the two beds. A shout rings out: "There are people in here!"

Immediately after that, the door of the room next to ours is forced open. I think about putting my hands up, like I've seen done so many times in films, but I cannot let go of my mother. Two killers come in. Another shout resounds: "There's a White girl here!" They force us to stand up and lead us outside to the mob. And there again: "There's a White girl!" All eyes are fixed on me.

They start asking questions: "Who are you, how long have you been here?" I watch the words flow from their large mouths, stinking rumbles that seem to come from a long way off. My mother's voice and the other woman's make the sound of tinkling bells. The men who had been hiding us until now are standing there, behind the killers. The cook is holding his head in his hand, overwhelmed. The gardener seems calmer. I do not immediately see, in the background, the bodies of the two young Tutsi hotel employees who have just been killed after being dragged out of the basement where they were hiding. My eyes stay strangely dry although I feel as if I am drowning; they are held fast by the shirt of a small man standing a little to my left. It must once have been light blue and white gingham. But now it is a dirty red and looks stiff, like cardboard. That shirt must have soaked up an enormous amount of blood these last few days, drying, then getting soaked over and over again, one massacre after another. It looks now like an old steak. And then there are his hands, holding firmly to strange weapons. A long and old kitchen knife in one, a kebab skewer in the other. Both of them covered in fresh blood.

The man in the gingham shirt has an amused expression on his face. Not threatening, not angry. No, amused. Well now, what a find, we thought we would dig up a few Tutsi cockroaches to crush here and now we discover a little White girl. I am something of an attraction, but because the kebab skewer is pressed on my neck, and it would not take much for it to be stuck into me, I understand that the amusement of my presence could rapidly turn into a morbid game. How does one kill a White Tutsi? As easily as a Black Tutsi?

For a long moment, I stay silent. Coming out onto the room's porch has dazzled me. We have been in the semi-darkness of our hiding place for several days. And then there is the ruckus of the excited voices of the killers, their gesticulations. They are surrounding us, weapons already drawn, set to cut us, to stab us, to crush us. The sun is high in the sky, my back is icy with sweat.

* * *

I do not know what the triggering element was. Maybe my mother's open purse, in which she is looking for the identity card they are demanding. That little pale green piece of cardboard, where, underneath a photograph with a fixed stare that they will only have to lift up, next to the heading UBWOKO-ETHNICITY, are the following words:

~~HUTU~~ – TUTSI – ~~TWA~~

We all know, after three years of the propaganda of hate, that the first move of anyone who says "Show me your I.D." to the people on all the hills of Rwanda is to lift up the identity photograph.

I can't remember whether she has already handed them the card or if she is shaking too much to find it in her bag, unless she was delaying the moment, naively hoping that something would happen, that something would put off our imminent death.

* * *

An idea is starting to take form in my mind, an island in the middle of the tempest.

* * *

The schoolchildren to whom I tell this story a quarter-century later ask me: "But how did you come up with the idea? Was it a tactic you had worked out beforehand?"

I answer that this is probably what you call survival instinct. Then I add: "I had not worked anything out, but I had always been interested in world news." That's the opportunity for me to talk to them about the virtues of curiosity, for me to encourage them to read "serious" newspapers, to diversify their sources of information. That is part of why I am there, so that my experience can allow their teachers later to give them the keys to understanding the world around them, so that they can become open-minded citizens capable of thinking for themselves.

I tell them my mother always loved listening to the news. Three times a day, in two languages and on three, sometimes four, different radio stations: Radio Rwanda, Radio Burundi, *Radio France Internationale* and sometimes the Voice of America. That at the time I thought this was excessive, and that the radio had become a problematic issue between us, to the point that the present I got for my fifteenth birthday was a radio-cassette player all of my own, so that I could listen to music, nothing but music. But I added that I still listened to a news bulletin along with her, because her habits had ended up becoming mine too.

* * *

In the spring of 1994, I therefore have a few notions of what is going on in the country politically, despite my young age, and I know that France is an important supporter of the genocidal government. It is that knowledge that compels me to put on the act I do. When I understand that we are about to be killed, that my mother's identity card will be the green light for our execution, I decide to pretend to be French. Because I do not want to be reduced to that Rwandan identity card, I make French, the language I have mastered since childhood thanks to my education at the Belgian international school, my new passport.

I open my mouth, raise my eyebrows, and talk to my mother in French, as loudly as my terrorised voice and the kebab skewer pointed under my chin allow: "What are they saying? I do not understand what they are saying, Maman!"

She is nonplussed for a moment, but the blood-covered hands are starting to grab my mother's bag and the face of the man in the gingham shirt has a butcher's smile on it.

I speak even louder and look at the man I identify as the leader of the gang: "I do not understand Kinyarwanda. Do you speak French?"

* * *

How did I guess who the leader was? Was it because he was the only one unarmed, the only one who was clean, wearing an impeccably ironed shirt, without a trace of blood, and with the top of a ballpoint pen poking out of his breast pocket?

* * *

I think there are about ten of them, maybe fifteen. These men have certainly macheted so many Tutsi since the beginning of the genocide that they have lost count. Yes, men, not animals, not monsters, but sons, fathers, husbands who will later go home and say to their mothers, their ageing fathers or their wives: "We did good work today." And there we are, three women, with me still very young, almost still a child, caught in the trap of their eyes, in the circle of violence they are forming around us, and dehumanised for so long by their language, by their hate built on propaganda and racist poison. And I am setting myself apart by saying: "I do not understand your language." I could say: "Why are you doing this?" A why which they would answer, like a Nazi did in other times: "Here there is no why." But I must have the sense that this question would not save us here. What I am saying, by taking refuge in the French language, is this: "I am not here to ask questions or to refute the meaning or the morality of your actions. No. I belong elsewhere and what you are doing here is none of my concern." And the chief of the horde – it is him alright – accepts my message. He must feel that he is granted authority by this language that only he can understand. He is an intellectual. When he speaks, I sense that the others take a step back so that he can answer me, as if to indicate their respect. We begin a conversation. My mother has understood my stratagem and acquiesces to what I am doing. And I gain more assurance with every sentence I utter.

He asks me how I can be French, pointing to my Tutsi mother, and I declare full of confidence that my father is French. Why is he not here? I say that he is in France and I was supposed to go and join him when the war broke out. But that father I invented on the spur of the moment has to be given flesh and blood, has to be made real for my interrogator.

So I take the address book out of my mother's still open bag. I know that we have several contacts in France, but their names are mostly written as couples, Monsieur and Madame So-and-so. The only one for whom there is only a man's name is the brother-in-law of Christine, the French nun who is my mother's friend. He came to Rwanda with Christine's sister and her husband, a few years earlier, and he decided, as they had, to sponsor me. He is married but because his wife did not accompany him during the journey, only his name is written in the address book. I point it out, and it seems that by this mere gesture he has appeared before us and I am introducing him to the leader of the pack. There, that's my father, you see, there's even his address there.

I think that is the moment I understand that my lie has been believed. I also say something like "François Mitterrand is your friend. If you kill a French citizen he will be angry and will stop helping you." It's almost a threat. I have nothing left to lose. I am aware of current events, I have heard about that famous back page of the Hutu extremist newspaper, on which the portrait of François Mitterrand was captioned: "A real friend of Rwanda".

* * *

When I tell this story to school students, I explain: "You never know what might save you. But having some knowledge of the world in which you are growing up, about the men and women who are your leaders, or more widely about the political issues of the day, can be useful. Never forget that."

I also tell them that doing good deeds can be helpful too, even if there are no guarantees, and I tell them about a young man, a penniless guy living in Butare doing odd jobs or begging, to whom my mother sometimes gave a little money for him to pump up our bicycle tyres, and that day, having followed the killers like a travelling show, he detached himself from the pack to tell the others: "I know them, yes, she is actually French." He had not the slightest idea of the nationality of my father, but that day, he acted as our guarantor, maybe out of gratitude or maybe simply because this statement gave him a certain standing in the scene being played out, when he had never been more than a beggar.

I also explain to the children that thousands of Tutsi were massacred by neighbours for whom they had done many favours, some of whom were longstanding friends, that teachers had been raped and hacked to death by pupils they had taught to read and write, and that any and all past goodwill was worth nothing to the killers, who were not monsters, not animals, but determinedly amnesiac. Citizens transformed in the space of a few years by effective propaganda. I warn the students: "Do not think that propaganda only works on mostly illiterate African peasants, do not forget the Nazi system was able to take hold of the minds of many European intellectuals, look at how neo-fascist discourse is gaining ground in the French media today, ask yourselves about the political convictions of the owners of some television channels, newspapers and publishing houses. Right here, right now. We must always remain vigilant."

* * *

After a discussion that seems both quick and interminable, the chief of the pack – to whom I have explained that the other woman hiding with us is my aunt, in order to put her under the protection of my tissue of lies – decrees that we should not be killed.

He tells me there is still a French man in the city, François Pigeot,[6] *and that he will go to find him to inform him of our presence. I pretend to know him, which again is part lie. I do not know him personally, but I know who he is: the proprietor of the garage across from the military camp in Butare, a forty- or fifty-year-old man who used to hang out with the French soldiers. He came to dinner once at the home of the Belgian family in Kigali where I board during the school terms.*

As he is preparing to leave, the leader of the pack gives us a telephone number on which he can be contacted and tells us to call him if we have any trouble.

* * *

Years later, I found that scrap of paper – with his name and the number we never dialled – among some of my old documents: Gérard 30 099.

* * *

He tells us he is a student at the University of Nyakinama, near Ruhengeri. I would find out later that the authorities brought northerners, who were much more extremist, down to the south to "get the work done".

The horde has left, leaving us trembling and partly relieved. It is at that moment, I think (but time was then distorted), that I see the bodies of the two slaughtered young men. I knew them both. One of them shared our hiding place for a time in the old cinema. It is the first time I have seen a dead body, I have no idea what to do. No-one seems to know. I pick some flowers growing on a nearby bush and lay them at their feet, avoiding looking at their faces and the wounds all over their bodies.

* * *

With hindsight, I can see that my gesture was childish, almost ridiculous, but at that moment I know I had to make some kind of arrangement with death, to try to keep it at bay.

Later I would find out that the two young men who managed to escape the horde were found and brought back to the hotel to be killed there too. I did not understand why they were not killed where they were found, in the woods, on the other side of the hotel's southern wall. Why bring them back to their hiding place? Unless the story I was told was incorrect or I confused it with another.

Passing time erodes memories, and the various stories, those heard, read or seen in documentaries, get mixed up together. My memory has perfectly fixed some moments and blurred others.

During the attack, the Hutu gardener of the hotel had a slightly devious look in his eyes, and he did nothing to try to defend us from the killers. Once the storm was past, once we were safe, we would think about his attitude and suspect in the end that it was he or his father who had denounced us.

I do not try to find extenuating circumstances for them, but I ask the students, who seem to be plunged into deep incomprehension: "How easy do you think it is, to become a righteous person?" One day war breaks out and you open your door to fugitives, motivated by a simple spirit of solidarity, because you cannot accept that they should die just like that, because you are convinced that it is the right thing to do. Little by little you come to understand that you have taken risks by helping them, that those who want to kill them can go after you as well, and that you have to provide food daily for the people you are hiding, and sometimes share your house with them where there may not be much space, and your meals were already frugal. You can do that for a week or so, or a month, but then what? Wouldn't you come to regret having taken a stand, if the war lasts longer than expected – can you ever know, when war breaks out, how long it will last? – and wouldn't you wish they would go away and leave you with your bread? Then you think that when they are dead, your brothers will no longer see you as weak.

In Rwanda, a few Hutu were killed because they refused to give up the Tutsi they were hiding. By comparing accounts of survivors, it became clear that often the men who were hiding family or friends in their houses would also go to kill at a roadblock not far away, so as not to arouse suspicion.

That is why there were so few righteous people in the end, people who held the line of goodness the whole way through, who refused to participate in the massacres from start to finish.

Three months is not a long time. But in that season of blood, each day seemed to last an eternity.

I am not trying to justify or forgive anyone, I am just trying to lay my anger down somewhere so that I can live without the weight of bitterness.

What would you have done in their place?

The children protest vehemently. Of course not! I would not have betrayed you.

I tell myself that's something at least. They will have asked themselves the question once in their youth, if they ever find themselves having to make that kind of choice. Can one prepare oneself to be righteous? Is goodness a matter of education? Rwanda has given the lie to so many convictions. Those who were helped by the Hutu fathers during the pogroms against the Tutsi in the 1960s and '70s turned to the sons, thinking that their fathers' benevolent attitude had been passed down, but ended up being killed. To each generation its morality. I can only hope that the old saying about skipping a generation will put the grandsons in the camp of the saviours and that education will do the rest in the meantime.

During my presentation in Nice in November 2022, a student asks me rather abruptly: "But why didn't you defend yourselves?" I volley the question back at him: "And how do you think we could have done that?" "With knives you had at home, spears or hunting weapons."

I tell him and his classmates about the decades of indoctrination, about how the Tutsi had become second-class citizens, but also how, in a prefecture like Butare, the families who had intermarried and tried to look past ethnicity (for, after all, the Hutu and Tutsi had always had the same language, the same religion, the same culture, and had always lived on the same territory, there was only one Rwandan ethnicity) had developed trust. I talk to them about the French Jews who told themselves: "I am French, I fought for my country, it won't let me down." I tell them that we trusted the international community, because there were "peacekeeping forces" stationed in the country. And then I tell them that when it all started, kitchen knives were of no use to us, I told them about the paralysis of fear, about the fact that the expression "mass killing" in this case means not only masses of victims but also masses of killers. They attacked in packs, coming in groups of ten, twenty, fifty.

The school clock is ticking, and I do not have time to tell them about those who tried to resist, the Tutsi in the chain of hills of Bisesero, armed with worn spears and rocks gathered by women and the elderly, about the man who was the head of that movement because he had experienced the resistance to the pogroms of 1959, 1962 and 1973, Aminadabu Birara, who organised men so that the families, gathered on the hilltops, could push back the killers armed with machetes. They held firm until May 13. That day, the attackers came back with soldiers. What can a spear or bow do against a Kalashnikov? A handful survived until June, until the arrival of the French *Opération Turquoise*, which abandoned them to the killers for three long days before returning.[7] I do not have time to talk about all of that, but I do hope, at the end of my presentation, that they understand the processes of domination that create victims, in the long or short term.

I talk about impunity and the culture of violence. And because the feminist that I am wants to make them understand the mechanisms that are common to different kinds of oppression, I draw a parallel with rape culture. All those times that a woman who has been raped is asked: "Why didn't you fight back?"

June 7, 1994. We are still here, in the courtyard in front of the hotel room, our hiding place uncovered, having survived, for now, when a soldier arrives. Fear and panic again. He has a gun at his belt. He has approached without making any noise, unless we were too overwhelmed to notice him coming, but he is there all of a sudden and asking us who we are. The adults explain, but he clearly doesn't see how being the daughter of a Frenchman should make me untouchable. He soon stops listening to the others and looks pointedly at me.

* * *

How old was he? I have no idea, but he was relatively young. I've forgotten his features, along with those of all the other killers. If I were to cross paths with him in the street today, I would not recognise him.

* * *

He is a simple soldier, but Karoli addresses him as "sergeant" or "captain" to flatter him. He looks at me with terrifying insistency, his nostrils dilated. Half his face is covered with a strange rash. Again the sea is stormy in my head. He tells me to go into the hotel room and puts his hand to his belt. I can see a chasm opening up in my mother's eyes and I understand. I repeat my stratagem, I pretend not to understand his language and my mother starts begging him, weeping, and trying to interpose herself between him and me. The shaking that takes over my body at that moment has remained a mystery to me. How can I stay standing when I am nothing more than an envelope of skin filled with swirling water? His belt is completely undone, he is starting to get impatient. I don't know exactly what he wants to do to me in the hotel room but I know that it is terrible, for I have heard what people have been whispering since the beginning of the genocide: "bamukoreye ibya mfura mbi", "baramurongoye" or "baramuhohoteye".

* * *

Even now I wonder how our language has always used such euphemisms to talk about rape. The first expression is very difficult to translate. "*Imfura*" is a term that means someone noble of heart, and in contrast "*imfura mbi*" means "the bad *imfura*". The literal meaning of the expression would therefore be something like "bad man things happened to her". The second term is even more baffling for it means "to get married". There is also the verb "*kubohoza*", close to "*kubohora*", but whereas the latter means to liberate, the former was used to describe gang rapes, which were legion at the time.

* * *

That day he is alone and I try, while standing perfectly still, to face his feverish stare. A few weeks earlier, our French teacher, who was giving a class about theatre, taught us the expression deus ex machina, *which I found appealing. At this precise moment, while I am claiming in French not to understand the language of this man who intends to violate me, this is the expression that floats in on the waves of my coast of madness, that scrap of Latin from the time when a drama was only something played by actors on stage. I clutch at it as at a lifebelt, so as not to hear what is about to take place. It is impossible that the fact of thinking about something in one's head should make it happen, and yet a moment later, there it is, my deus ex machina. While this very real scene is being played out, in the wings, the hotel waiter has rushed out onto the main street of Butare, to where he knows there are other military units stationed, and is calling for help.*

* * *

All that. As I am writing this. Seems so unreal. And yet. It happened. An unbelievable stroke of luck that few people had in those days of ash.

* * *

The waiter, Vénuste, comes back with a P.G., a presidential guard, one of those who are at the top of the hierarchy of soldiers, and no doubt informs him of the story the gang was passing around as he left, that there is a French girl there and that their chief has gone to get the White garage owner to come to collect her. I do not know how all of this plays out, but the P.G. arrives and signals to the soldier who is about to rape me in the hotel room that he should leave us alone. It is over.

I sit down on a low wall and listen to the waves recede in my head.

* * *

In 2003, nine years later, this story came back to me in an unexpected way. I was the coordinator of a project with *Médecins sans Frontières* fighting the A.I.D.S. epidemic in Douala, in Cameroon. One evening as I was reading, sitting on the terrace of our apartment, located on the Carrefour Armée de l'Air, after a day at work, my colleague and flatmate, a young Italian virologist, came home and was visibly impatient to show me something. He had spent the afternoon examining patients with H.I.V. at the Congo II health centre, in the New Bell district, a poor neighbourhood where the N.G.O. was working. He had taken photographs and I imagine he saw them as proof that he was at last working in the field, that the theoretical cases he had learned about at university in Milan had been transformed before his very eyes, into real patients. "I have to show you this, Beaaata!" – he had a strange way of lengthening some of the vowels in French that he had learned from his Sephardic grandmother. Alessandro had a digital camera, a rare piece of equipment at the time. And that is when I saw again, on his screen, the skin of the soldier who almost raped me. It was just the same, apart from the shape of his face, his eyes and his mouth; it was the same rash covering half his face from his ear to his chin, raised red spots filled with liquid and starting to form small lesions on his skin.

"Look at these amazing facial shingles, I've never seen anything like it!" The doctor was in raptures, and I was just realising what I had escaped.

I have since read that an estimated 250,000 Tutsi women were raped during the genocide, and that there was a deliberate policy of having those crimes committed by men with H.I.V. I heard that some rapists decided not to kill their victims and left them on the ground saying: "What I've given you will kill you slowly." Before the genocide, Rwanda was one of the African countries most affected by the virus, notably with more than a quarter of the population of Kigali being contaminated.

It was when I was working for M.S.F. Switzerland in Cameroon that the trials at the International Criminal Tribunal for Rwanda started in Arusha. I remember the boundless rage I felt when I found out that the presumed genocidal men who were there and had H.I.V. were receiving triple therapy funded by the United Nations, whereas the women who had been raped were effectively being left to die in Rwanda because of the still insufficient access to healthcare there. I remember that my rage was also provoked by what came out of some of the sessions, where women who had the huge courage to come forward and bear witness to the rapes they endured were challenged by lawyers with cruel violence, and accused of lying because, so they said, in the conditions of the genocide, they undoubtedly had not been able to wash for days, and it was unlikely that those men would have wanted them.

* * *

June 7, 1994. Late afternoon. Some time has passed. The French garage owner arrives. I tell him the same story. For more credibility, I also tell him I am the niece by marriage of Sister Christine, the French nun whose family was sponsoring me. He knows her, as he does all the French people in Butare, since he is a block warden, charged by the French embassy with the evacuation of French citizens in case of trouble. At that moment he seems to believe the story I am telling and says he will take me to the premises of the bishopric where I will be safe. He cannot take my mother or the other woman right now, but he promises to come back and get them. And this time, I abandon my mother. They have the telephone number of the student leader of the militia and assure me they will call him if they need to. Does the hotel telephone even work?

The Frenchman hardly says a word to me in his pick-up truck, as I climb in with my little escape bag, the one with my school reports and my photograph album. He seems annoyed at having to deal with my situation. But the premises of the bishopric are only five minutes' drive away from the hotel where we were hiding, and it is all over in the blink of an eye. As we take the road leading down to the Buye neighbourhood, through the truck window I can see a roadblock, a dead tree trunk set on barrels, a gang of armed men with beer bottles in their hands. The sun is starting to set.

I spend the night in the apartment of a German nun who works for the bishopric, Maria Utler. She knows me well. I think she even taught at the lycée my mother attended in Save during the 1960s. My sleep is disturbed by brutal awakenings and tormented dreams. I wonder if I will find my mother alive in the morning.

I lose track of time, I have no idea if it is morning or afternoon the next day when Pigeot returns. He brings good news, another deus ex machina: "Sister Christine arrived in Butare today."

A few White members of religious orders who were evacuated from Butare to Burundi in mid-April have been granted permission by the genocidal authorities to make regular journeys back to the city to bring supplies to those in their orders who have not been able to leave the country.

"Sister Christine is at the Karubanda school, I'll take you to her."

What about my mother?

"I'll go and get her straight after that to take her there too."

And again, his pickup truck, a trip of barely a few kilometres, again passing a roadblock where he doesn't have to stop, he seems to be well known to all the militiamen, he can move around the city without the least difficulty.

* * *

Years later, I did some research about him, to try to understand what he was doing there. It seems he might have been a secret agent. The only trace of him that my husband and I could find on the internet was the fact that he was made *Chevalier de l'ordre du Mérite*, at the request of the Ministry for Cooperation, by a decree dated May 1994 (in the middle of the genocide!). For "29 years of professional activity and military service". It appears he was evacuated from Butare on July 3 by *Opération Turquoise*, in other words the same day as the last convoy by *Terre des Hommes*, but in his case it was to the *Turquoise* zone close to the Congo border, where the government and the genocidal army also took refuge.

* * *

When I arrive at the Karubanda school, Sister Christine, who has known me forever, hugs me in silence. She and François Pigeot head towards the centre of the school and the dormitories, which have been transformed into a reception centre for children under the direction of Terre des Hommes. There is a crowd of people there. I follow closely in their wake, fearing I'll be left behind. At that point I hear the garage owner say to the nun: "Apparently her father is not French at all, and you are not at all related. Someone told me her father is Polish." My heart stops. I know that she said something to him, a sentence whose exact words I have forgotten, but in which she asks him to help us, and she will vouch for me. He replies: *"Well, I've already done the paperwork anyway."* He then gives me a sheet of white paper. The letterhead bears the seal of the French Embassy in Rwanda, with typed underneath: *"I the undersigned, François Pigeot, representative of the Embassy of France in Rwanda, hereby declare that Beata Umubyeyi is the daughter of . . . residing in . . . and must return to France as soon as possible to the care of her father. Etc."*

He explains to Christine how he fiddled with the stamp of the French school in Butare, by cutting out its name, leaving only the rest: *"Embassy of France in Rwanda"*.

Then he goes to collect my mother. While I am waiting for him, a young P.E. teacher from another school, the Groupe Scolaire, *who is one of the onlookers there*, recognises me. I am suspicious when he asks me, with a contrite air: *"Oh, Beata, thank God you are here, but where is your mother?"* I pretend to be grieving and whisper: *"She was killed."*

Until she has come to join me here in the Karubanda school, I want to be sure that no-one will go and assassinate her where I abandoned her.

Christine gives me a change of clothes and takes me to a young woman who is looking after the children gathered there. She tells me that she has to go back to Burundi, but that she will do whatever she can to get us out of there. I will see her only a month later, in France.

*

I get taken to one of the dormitory cubicles with mattresses on the ground. Claire, a girl two years older than I am, greets me and shows me my bed. She introduces her sisters who are occupying the other beds with her. They take me under their wing from the first day and explain how the centre works.

Later on, the woman to whom Sister Christine introduced me when I arrived comes to get me discreetly and takes me to a closed door on which she gently knocks. When the door opens, I see my mother again. We fall into each other's arms and there again I do not cry. She is being hidden in the room that used to be occupied by the night monitor who looked after the dormitory when the lycée students slept there. She will stay there, without going out, until our departure on June 18.

My mother is getting thinner and thinner. In a corner of the room is a shower with a bucket of water. She washes my long hair, which has not been washed for almost two months. The water is cold, it can't be wasted. Then I go back to live with the other children in the dormitory. When night falls suddenly at around 6 p.m., as it does every day there, we lie down on our mattresses and tell each other stories of our escape and of our dead. Claire is the oldest of five girls who managed to survive by taking refuge with their aunt who is married to a Swiss man, who brought them to Terre des Hommes before being evacuated himself.

Their father and mother were killed.

At night, the youngest children cry a lot, you can hear a few of them having nightmares until first light. Some of the children are wearing huge bandages on their heads *or arms. Arms they raised to protect themselves from a blow from a machete or a club. I am told that the children were brought here by people who had hidden them for a while or picked them up while they were still clinging to their parents' corpses. I am told that some of the children were orphans before the massacres, both Hutu and Tutsi, and that they fled from the armed fighting in Kigali with their carers. There are also the physically handicapped adolescents who were living in the Gatagara re-education centre, near Nyanza, who have been evacuated here.*

The injured children mostly have traumatic mutism; their eyes are frozen. They stay sitting or lying down, immobile. Others cry without stopping until sleep takes them. Some of them are unbearably thin and their hair has gone stringy and red.

I only leave the dormitory to go to collect my daily food rations. Outside, in front of the door of what was once the school library, there are always people from the city, military or civilians: they come to see who is there. Some of them obviously regret not being able to kill us on the spot.

One afternoon, a young woman is carried into the dormitory, to the cubicle next to mine. She is unconscious. She was picked up in front of the school, on the main road, behind the eucalyptus trees. Her skirt is soiled with blood around her lower abdomen. I do not know how many militiamen or soldiers ravaged her. I stay listening to her groans for hours, paralysed by the idea of what irreparable damage they have done to her. I never discover her name. She dies the next day without having said a word.

*

THE TENSE OF TESTIMONY

Around a week later, I have to go and join my mother in her hiding place, for a rumour about me has started to circulate through the group of vultures crowded in front of the library. Some of them are gossiping that I am the daughter of the minister Landoald Ndasingwa (Lando); they think that I escaped the massacre of his family and found refuge here. There is a risk they may come and find me to take me away and kill me, in the eucalyptus wood or elsewhere.

Lando was the founder and vice-president of one of the main opposition parties, the Liberal Party, and was also the only Tutsi minister in the transitional democratic government, most of whose members were killed in the first days of the genocide. His wife was Canadian and they had two mixed-race children. We found out that the whole family was massacred in Kigali. I know just who Lando's daughter is – she was called Malaïka, I think – because she and I went to the same Belgian school in Kigali. She was taller than me, curvier, and had short hair. We had nothing in common except our mixed-race skin, but of course the growing rumour mill could not care less about that. So I have to go once more into hiding.

The room where we spend our last days in Butare is equipped with a single bed, a mattress, sheets and blankets. An unaccustomed luxury. Someone brings us a little water and food every day. We are in much more comfortable conditions here than we previously were but have less contact with the outside world. The windows of this room are too high to allow us to see what is going on outside. Apart from the children's crying, all the noises are muffled. The future remains uncertain.

*

THE CONVOY

One morning, a group of foreigners comes to see us. I think there were three of them. In my memory I talk to them in English, translating for them what my mother says. Very soon afterwards, we are called: there is a convoy of trucks leaving for Burundi, we are going to join it.

When my mother and I leave our hiding place, the courtyard in front of the dormitory is crowded with people. Two large trucks are parked there, ready for a cargo of condemned humans. I do not remember how we got up there, I have vague images of outstretched hands pulling us and others pushing us, and then of settling at the very back of a container truck. The panels boom when you hit them. Grey blankets have been spread out to protect us from splinters from the wooden floor and to cover the dirt left behind by the various merchandise once carried in the vehicle to supply our small landlocked country from the distant ports of Mombasa and Dar es-Salaam. We have no commercial value. For the humanitarian workers we are a good deed, for the journalists a good story. But it may well be that the préfet *Nsabimana, who will accompany the convoy to be sure that we safely cross the border, it may well be that this man sees in us a possible transaction, a wager on the future. Your lives for mine. The wind is turning: soon his government and his genocidal army will be routed. And then it will be quite useful to be able to say: "I saved some Tutsi children."*

But for now the convoy is just taking off. One of the two heavy doors of the container remains partly open, held by a rope, so that we are not plunged into complete darkness, and to let in some air. I remember two White men, with light-coloured hair, standing next to the door from time to time. Later, when I see the images from the B.B.C., I discover that it was the sound recordist and the cameraman.

I lose track of time. The trucks and a few other small vehicles which constitute our convoy are jolting forwards. It will take us several hours to travel the thirty kilometres that separate Butare from the border. The road is bristling with roadblocks manned by the militia. Often they are just a tree trunk set across the road. Men armed with machetes, clubs and other lethal weapons control everything that goes on. I do not see any of those men, because each time we feel the truck slow down, my mother and I lie flat on our stomachs and cover ourselves with sheets and pieces of fabric and the smaller children sit on top of us. At each roadblock, the furious militiamen look into the truck, scanning the faces of the children, aware that there are many Tutsi among them who are escaping. Once we get to the border, we can no longer hide. Once again, anonymous arms reach out to help us down.

* * *

My memory of this moment is fragmented. Some of the scenes have stayed clearly etched in my memory, others remain vague. I have no idea, for instance, in what order things happened.

* * *

My heart goes wild and almost stops three times.

My mother sees a soldier drinking beer with another man. They are seated at a table in front of a little house that must be a sort of bar, looking out over the border post and the open space on which we have disembarked. She appears to recognise him and walks forwards, her eyes raised and her face tense. I am there, unaware of who this is. The man recognises us too, his eyes express surprise. He frowns and signals with a shake of his head that we should not approach him. It is only later that I understand what played out there. The soldier in question is Colonel Alphonse Nteziryayo. He comes from the same hill as my mother, so of course they know each other. At that moment, she knows nothing of the very active role this man has played in the extermination of the Tutsi where she comes from. When she sees him, she is probably thinking that this man can help us cross the border.

Why does he not have us killed on the spot? Is it because of the humanitarian workers and journalists present?

A soldier puts a gun to my mother's head. We are standing back somewhat from the rest of the crowd, I feel as if no-one is noticing what is going on. The man did not even ask for my mother's identity card, he must have decided on the basis of her features alone that she must die. Once again, the chasm in her eyes, the panicky feeling that it's all over now, just a few metres from salvation. Did the préfet *see this scene? I have no idea. I remember the sound the gun made, a click the significance of which I would understand only a few years later while watching a film in France. Once again, a* deus ex machina: *another soldier, perhaps an officer (was it Nteziryayo? Was it after this incident that my mother tried to approach him? Everything is mixed up in my memory) stops him, showing him the White journalists filming another scene close by.*

* * *

THE TENSE OF TESTIMONY

It is only later that I deduce that it was the presence of the reporters that saved us every time. No doubt also the humanitarian workers, even if I do find out that during the preceding convoy, they had not been able to prevent some adult Tutsi from being sent back to Butare.

I consider, after the fact, the power of those Westerners, who by their mere presence can save lives, at a time when the genocidal authorities are trying to enhance their reputation on the international scene. I can't help comparing the ridiculously small number of journalists present in Rwanda to the number of those – 2,500! – sent to cover the first free elections in South Africa.

I can't help ruminating over the now accepted idea that the genocide might have been stopped with no difficulty by the foreign military who came to evacuate the expats at the beginning of April (400 Belgian and 500 French nationals) if they had joined forces with the 2,500 U.N. peacekeeping troops present in the country at the time. The way the international community abandoned Rwanda is aptly summarised in this statement by a young French researcher, Florence Piton: "[. . .] those few thousand men would undoubtedly have encountered little difficulty in putting an end to the massacres in Kigali. [. . .] The stopping of the massacres in Kigali in the first few days would have restrained the killings in the rest of the country."

* * *

Was it before or after those scenes that my mother went to the border control office? I do not know. I vaguely remember a counter, and my mother handing over her passport, her hands shaking, the many eyes staring at us, the muffled voices of the dozens of children behind us whom the humanitarian workers were leading to the border post.

* * *

And then, as we are going to join them, I remember the préfet — how do I know it is him? We did not know him before 1994, maybe someone introduced us to him before we left Butare? — talking to us with a jovial air. He says to me in French: "So, are you happy now? You'll be able to go to see your father in France!" And without thinking I reply: "Yes! Murakoze cyane." ("Thank you very much" in Kinyarwanda.) The préfet's face stiffens for a moment and he says: "Hey, I was told you did not speak Kinyarwanda." And I panic and try to repair my mistake — what a shame to fail so close to our goal — by protesting and imitating the foreigners' accent when they speak our language: "Gakeh, gakeh." ("A bit, a bit.") That seems to satisfy him, and he wishes us bon voyage *(!), tells me not to forget my country over there and that he hopes I will come back to visit later. Listening to him, so nonchalant and cheerful, you'd think I was going to France for a student exchange, and not fleeing an extermination in which he himself — I was unaware of this at the time — has been actively participating.*

We shake his hand, thank him once again, and we join the group of children who have started to cross the border. Do we also thank the humanitarian workers from Terre des Hommes? *I would like to think we did, but I have no memory of doing so. My mother, weakened by more than two months of privations and anxiety, is by my side in her now baggy red tracksuit. I do not turn around. In front of us, on the other side of the barrier for entry into Burundi, there are many foreigners who have come with their vehicles, minibuses and pickup trucks to meet us. Some* of them are people originally from Butare, who were evacuated in April. A few of them recognise us and burst into tears as they hug our emaciated shoulders. "You're still alive!"

In this welcome committee is the Canadian nun from the same order as Sister Christine, who I pretended was my aunt, and Georges, a colleague of hers. They will drive us directly to Bujumbura, the capital, and from that point onwards we will have no more contact with Terre des Hommes. We will stay in Burundi for two weeks, long enough to get a visa for France.

During our stay in Bujumbura, we reconnect with my cousin Rafiki, who was able to leave her family hill on April 17. At that point, people thought that if Tutsi were being killed, it would mostly be educated city residents, as was the case in the previous pogroms. My cousin tells us how her father would wait anxiously at the side of the road leading to Butare, hoping that we would come and seek refuge in the countryside, where we would be safe. A few days later, the killings were pitiless throughout those very hills. And, how ironic, it was in town that we were able to survive: the city offered us hiding places that were unimaginable in rural areas. With two neighbouring high school students, Rafiki, disguised as a man, had found a boatman who was prepared to take them across the river that separates the south of Rwanda from Burundi, and finally, after innumerable difficulties, joined members of her extended family who had taken refuge in Burundi two decades earlier. At the time we do not know that none of her brothers and sisters, nor her parents, survived the killings. The news brought by those who were able to escape in extremis is appalling, but *we can't help hoping that our family members, perhaps, may have ...*

The tension is palpable in Bujumbura. The president of Burundi perished in the same plane crash which killed his Rwandan counterpart; a transitional government is being formed, but in the evenings shots often ring out in some neighbourhoods.

We leave on a night flight, on July 4. This is the first time in my life that I have been in a plane. Seeing my distress, the man sitting next to me, with greying hair and a slight British accent, tries to reassure me. We learn that he is the programme director for Terre des Hommes. *His name is Richard Copeland. To him at least, I clearly remember that we expressed our profound gratitude.*

We are met in Paris by Christine's sister and her husband, Chantal and Bernard Blondelle, who come to greet us at the airport.

They will become my French host family, both generous and caring.

* * *

The *préfet* Nsabimana will be stripped of his functions when he returns from the border. In an irony of fate, it is Alphonse Nteziryayo, the colonel whom we saw as we were crossing the border, who is appointed as his replacement and who will finish the massacre of the Tutsi in the area.

As for the B.B.C. crew, they return to Butare with the *préfet*, before leaving the country for good the very next day.

This is how, in the book he published a year later, Fergal Keane tells their experience of that evacuation and departure, which he blends into a single moment:

THE TENSE OF TESTIMONY

From the roadway it sounds like the chattering of little birds. There are many, many small voices, all of them babbling excitedly. In the park children from the age of two upwards are being organised into groups with numbers pinned to their clothes. The clothing is bright and new. Several aid workers go around reassuring the infants who are crying. People are very tense. On one recent convoy the Interahamwe seized several children from a truck and killed them. After all, the militiamen have been told not to repeat the mistake of 1959. Tutsi orphans are a prime target. Nsabimana arrives with an army officer and a civilian official. There is much toing and froing with the aid workers. Nsabimana goes to each of the three trucks and speaks to the children in Kinyarwanda.

David, Glenn and Tony climb into the lead lorry, and Rizu and I follow in the Land Rover. We are at the rear of the convoy. "Stay close to them. We do not want to get separated," I say. "I think I am able to drive, thank-you," she replies tartly. I apologise immediately. It is just my nervousness at the thought of those thirty roadblocks between Butare and the border. Even with Nsabimana there is no guarantee that the militia will wave the children through. Before we leave the doors of the trucks are partially closed. There is a sufficient gap to allow air in. Inside the children continue to talk to each other. I look inside the first truck and in the semi-dark see the wide eyes of the infants staring back at me. They are quiet for a few minutes, until I take my head away and the excited chatter begins again. The aid workers climb into the trucks. There is a Japanese photographer with them and he begins to sing nursery rhymes, encouraging the children to join in. With the voices high above the grumble of the trucks we head out onto the road and south towards Burundi.

Nsabimana's limousine moves in between the trucks, racing ahead every time we approach a roadblock. Rizu keeps the car almost glued to the last truck. We say very little to each other. The journey is too tense for conversation. All of our energy and will seems directed to the task of getting to the border without an incident. I wonder what we will do if they try and seize some children. The militia would kill us if we tried to intervene. But could we stand by and watch little innocents being dragged off to be butchered? Roadblock after roadblock. The same routine each time. Nsabimana stops, rolls down his window and begins the explanation. The sight of the army officer in his car placates the Interahamwe. But my heart stops when we reach the roadblock where the gendarme had interrogated us a few days previously. The men at this barrier are more numerous and well armed than any of the rest. Nsabimana's car stops. The trucks grind to a halt. From the front seat of the car I can see Glenn's blond head bobbing around near the door of the last truck. The Japanese photographer is sitting there as well talking to the children. A militiaman with a machete approaches the truck slowly. He walks around to the back door. Another man carrying a club joins him. There is sweat pouring down my forehead. Rizu coughs and taps her fingers on the steering wheel. The militiamen gaze into the truck, one after the other. Seconds stretch tortuously into minutes. Other Interahamwe are moving around the first and second trucks. Nsabimana is still talking. Then his hand appears out of the window of the car. He is waving us forward and the convoy starts up and once more rolls south. By the time we reach the border post both Rizu and I are beyond the stage of worry. I believe we have reached a stage of acceptance that allows us to move beyond fear and simply exist without thinking.

At the border Patrice (the Rwandan army sergeant escorting the journalists in the zone controlled by the genocidal government) is waiting with several other soldiers. He welcomes us like old friends and then goes to help with the lifting of the children down from the trucks. The children follow the instructions of the aid workers without complaint. Some of them slip into the bushes to answer the call of nature and then run back to their preassigned groups. The préfet is talking to the border guards, showing them his piece of paper and then sitting down to chat for a few minutes. When he comes back I ask him why he was willing to help the children.

"They should not be blamed for the problems of the adult world. I have my own children. I would not want to see this happening to them. A child is innocent. It has no say in what happens," he says. (Sylvan Nsabimana does not know that soon after he left for the border the military commander of Butare issued an instruction for his dismissal. Nsabimana was replaced by an army officer.) As we talk the procession of children moves towards the border. The older ones are holding the hands of the smaller ones. The aid workers carry the babies. They pause momentarily at the barrier, dip underneath, straightening up for their last footsteps out of Rwanda, and then walking quietly together up the road to Burundi. Somewhere behind them, lying in mass graves or pit latrines or burned-out houses, were the bodies of their parents. As I watch them enter Burundi and board the buses that have been lined up to take them to Bujumbura, I think of Frank Ndore (the R.P.F. officer escorting the crew in the zone controlled by the Tutsi rebels) and how he made the same journey back in 1959. I wish for all the world that he could be here, that he could greet these exiles and guide them away from the past. Right now I suppose Frank is with the R.P.F. forces advancing on the remnants of the government army. Frank and Valence are out there on the other side of the line. In a few weeks they will be in Butare. The town will have fallen easily. The rector and the vice-rector and all of Butare's Hutu elite will be gone along with the soldiers and the militiamen. The majority will head for Zaire, where Mobutu has offered sanctuary. Some will head for the "safe area" established by the French near the Zairean border. And when the French leave, having staved off a final rebel victory by a few months, the fleeing Hutus will move to Goma, where the genocidal regime has set up its headquarters in exile. Sylvan Nsabimana will flee to Nairobi and will find his name appearing in a list of people accused of complicity in the genocide. It is true that his period as préfet saw massive killings in the Butare region. He protests his innocence.

For now it is good enough to be leaving. This departure is like a benediction. Uplifting. I feel as if I am escaping from prison. I know the others feel exactly the same way. Glenn and Tony are joking and laughing. Rizu is talking about the meal we will have in Nairobi. And David, as ever, is guiding us along. He is jotting down "things to do" in his notebook and planning the editing of the film. At the Burundian passport control we sip warm beer. Glenn talks about the fish he is going to catch once he gets back to South Africa. Tony has plans to visit Japan with *his wife. Rizu is making a feature film in Zimbabwe. Not even the Burundian customs forcing us to unload all of our equipment can take away the sweet feeling of release. Rwanda is now the country behind us. It no longer lies down the road, a slowly unfolding nightmare. Our journey home has begun. It is impossible to tell you how good it feels.*

The journalists have left. The humanitarian aid workers will undertake one last evacuation, at the beginning of July.

The time has come at last for me to recount what I know about them and about the organisation of those improbable convoys, in the eye of the catastrophe.

3
Terre des Hommes

"They are not the heroes people would like to say they are now. They are human beings, and the living proof is that even in the worst situations, there will always be a grain of humanity burning. And it is for that grain that I will write.
So that it might live in you who will read this book."

Sur Vivantes
Esther Mujawayo (with Saouâd Belhaddad)

How do investigations advance? After more than a quarter-century, how was I supposed to find the strangers with whom I had shared the longest hours of my life, the particular day that brought us out of hell? My investigation was not at all linear, it progressed in jolts. There were disappointments and plot twists. It is still, as I write, not entirely finished.

This story is full of holes and dotted lines, like the memories of the survivors. It took me through moments of absolute doubt, it brought back childhood grief which I thought was buried, but it also offered me unforgettable encounters.

When I got home from Nice in 2019, I started searching with no particular method. First on the internet, with the help of Yann, my husband. I was pleasantly surprised to find several archival documents that mention the *Terre des Hommes* convoys. Some items from the trial of the International Criminal Tribunal for Rwanda were on an internet site, francegenocidetutsi.org, a veritable goldmine of archives, created and maintained for many years by two Frenchmen, Jacques Morel and Aymeric Givord.

That was where I first read the name of Alexis Briquet, the delegate of *Terre des Hommes* in Rwanda during the genocide. I had no precise memory of this man at the time. During the evacuation, I saw several White people around us, but knew nothing of their role, much less their names. I was fifteen and terrified. All I knew was that these people were part of an organisation called *Terre des Hommes* and were there to help us. In the decades since then, when anyone asked me how I managed to escape the country in the middle of the genocide, I said that it was thanks to that N.G.O. I spoke about it as a single entity which contained all the individuals whose faces I had forgotten.

Since discovering Alexis Briquet's name, I have often wondered about the anonymisation that I imposed on our rescuers. That unconsciously created imprecision. It was probably because I had not talked directly with them, and because no-one introduced them by name or explained their roles.

By discussing this with a few children from the convoys with whom I had made contact, I understood that it was the same for them too. We had not spent enough time with the Swiss humanitarian aid workers or the two Italian journalists who accompanied them to have known or remembered their names. Later on, when I read the mission reports and the extracts from the deposition of Alexis Briquet at the International Criminal Tribunal, I realised that those humanitarian aid workers were mostly based in Burundi and only made return trips of two or three days to Butare, which also reduced the time they spent with the children.

After the genocide, I had learned the names of other humanitarian aid workers and rescuers. The ones the media talked about. I retained the name of Philippe Gaillard, the head of the I.C.R.C. (the International Committee of the Red Cross), who, with his medical and logistics team, had kept a hospital open in Kigali during the three months of killings. I probably remembered that name because Gaillard had given interviews that I later found in various books and documentaries on the subject. At the genocide memorial in Kigali, which I visited on my first trip back to the country in 2005, I had seen the portrait of Carl Wilkens, an American working for the Seventh-Day Adventist Church, who had refused to be evacuated with the other expats and had helped people hiding in the city of Kigali by supplying them with food and water. The number of foreigners who stayed or came back to rescue the Tutsi, when all the others were evacuated, was tiny, barely twenty in the entire country, and mostly humanitarian aid workers or members of religious orders.

With the exception of one reference in the book *Leave None to Tell the Story: Genocide in Rwanda* by Alison Desforges, published in 1999 for Human Rights Watch, the people from *Terre des Hommes* had left without a trace. Or left traces so faint that I had never noticed them before. And that is how, in my mind, the organisation had taken on the form of an almost abstract entity.

When, at the age of 22, freshly graduated with a master's in international cooperation and humanitarian action from the Sorbonne, I had searched for a position that would allow me to go to work in my home country, I had spontaneously turned to the I.C.R.C. and to *Médecins sans Frontières* (M.S.F.). I supported the stance taken by M.S.F., in which they had denounced the collusion of the French state with the regime responsible for the massacres, declaring in 1994: "You do not stop a genocide with doctors." I was filled, perhaps far too romantically, as one can be at that age, with a feeling of gratitude towards those two organisations who had not abandoned us during the genocide.

Why had I not thought of proposing my services to *Terre des Hommes*? That is a mystery I cannot explain to myself.

So, at 22, I was hoping to go back to work in Rwanda. After a few disappointments with my applications, I finally received an explanation from a well-meaning employee of the I.C.R.C.: "N.G.O.s don't send people to the places they are originally from. It is believed that they won't be able to show the neutrality required in responsible positions, unlike expatriates." I would mull over this strange policy for a long time to come.

It was M.S.F. Switzerland who finally hired me to work in a programme fighting A.I.D.S. in Cameroon, a country about which I knew virtually nothing, but where I was considered able to be neutral and impartial. That first posting lasted three months, in other words around the same length of time that Alexis spent in my country in 1994. I remember how as I walked in the streets of Yaoundé every day to go to work, neighbours would greet me by calling me "*Sans Frontière*". When you do not stay long, and the direct benefactors of your work are mostly children or teenagers, it is no wonder that nobody remembers your name.

When I started my research on the internet in 2019, the first documents I found indicated that an accord had been signed between the Swiss N.G.O. and the Rwandan Ministry of Social Affairs in May 1994, authorising the evacuation of 2,000 children to neighbouring Zaire (now the Democratic Republic of Congo). It was jointly signed by Alexis Briquet and the Italian Consul to Rwanda, Pierantonio Costa. I also found two press articles published after the last convoy, at the beginning of July, as well as, rather improbably, an interview with the captain of the Rwandan basketball team, who said that he had survived the genocide of the Tutsi thanks to a convoy organised by *Terre des Hommes*. I immediately contacted the young man via Instagram messaging, and, as I had done previously with Rodrigue, offered to send him the four photographs in my possession and asked him if he was part of the convoy on June 18. To begin with he seemed interested, although he was very busy, and gave me his e-mail address so I could send him the photographs, but he never responded when I did. I was puzzled. Would these photographs be of interest to the other children? I imagined that it would not be easy to find them. Was it worth the trouble?

In March 2020, a young, self-assured president of France announced on television that the French people were at war. I said to myself that he had no idea what he was talking about. Three months went by. The peculiar experience of the Covid pandemic had shifted something inside me. The interminable weeks of total lockdown that we went through prompted me to start a proper research project, beyond the few traces that were available online at the time.

As fate would have it, Bertille Descamps, a friend from my teenage years, one of the first friends I made in high school when I arrived in the north of France in 1994, was then working in the human resources department of *Terre des Hommes* in Lausanne.

That was how, in the beginning of the summer of 2020, I asked her to put me in touch with the archivist of the N.G.O.

The first response I received from him immediately made me understand that my request had a very slim chance of succeeding. He started by explaining that *Terre des Hommes* had given its oldest archives to the archival service of the Swiss canton of Vaud. Only the sources that were older than thirty years and did not refer to specific persons were available in free access. This was unfortunately not the case with the archives relating to the operations undertaken during the Rwandan genocide. He also wrote that the legitimacy of my request would be tempered by their duty to protect the privacy of the people whose personal data was referred to in the sources. He therefore did not have the right to give me the names of the children who were in my convoy, nor those of the employees of *Terre des Hommes* who organised it, without first obtaining their consent to be contacted. And he also recognised that, since the N.G.O. did not keep up-to-date contact information for anyone once the aid missions were over, he could not guarantee that he would be able to find these people to ask for their agreement.

I understood that data protection was taken very seriously by the N.G.O., which was actually a good thing. But how was I going to make any progress, when it was in fact those very names and contacts that I was looking for?

My correspondent nevertheless suggested that he could consult the files in the archives of the canton of Vaud relating to the Rwandan operations in 1994, in order to check whether any information existed about the convoy that crossed the border on June 18, 1994, and which parts of it could be shared with me.

When he contacted me again two weeks later, he only confirmed what I already knew: that there was indeed a convoy on June 18, and that it was Alexis Briquet who organised four convoys. He told me that, according to the mission reports he had read, a total of more than 1,000 children were evacuated.

Finally, he told me that he did not find in the archives any lists of the children who were part of the convoys, and explained that these lists probably stayed in Rwanda to cover organisational and operational requirements during the mission and were then transferred to the agencies who took on the activities of *Terre des Hommes* when they left the country in 1995.

As I read his message, I thought, rather bitterly, that my investigation had not got me very far.

But the last paragraph of his message gave me faint hope. The archivist informed me that one of his colleagues, Ariane Zwahlen, who was still on the staff in Lausanne, was a delegate for *Terre des Hommes* in Rwanda in 1994. He said that she had willingly agreed to talk to me to give me a first-hand account of her experience of those events.

We quickly agreed to a video call and this woman would thus give me a summary of the presence of the N.G.O. in the country, before, during and after the genocide. In parallel, I conducted some online research about the history of the organisation.

I found out that *Terre des Hommes* was founded in 1960 by Edmond Kaiser, a French Jew and former Resistance fighter who had settled in Switzerland after World War II.

It was during the battle for Algerian independence that he organised the first convoy of children, before setting up interventions with children threatened by the wars in Vietnam, Biafra, Cambodia and other countries. A charismatic personality, Kaiser often appeared in the Swiss media and was notorious for the many virulent telexes he used to send to world leaders to denounce human rights violations. Kaiser left *Terre des Hommes* in 1980 to found another N.G.O., *Sentinelles*, which would also care for injured Rwandan children, as Révérien Rurangwa relates in his account *Génocidé*, as well as for orphaned children to be adopted.

On the site of the Swiss radio and television service, R.T.S., I found an interesting archival document, dating from June 19, 1994: a special event to raise funds for *Sentinelles*. The evening programme included a live broadcast from a studio where people on telephones received calls from donors, appearances by celebrities like the singer Marc Lavoine, who performed on set, eyewitness accounts by volunteers from *Sentinelles*, and a rambling interview with Edmond Kaiser, who called for his compatriots to adopt children. He had invited the director of the Federal Office for Foreigners, who agreed to provide support for the legal procedures for these adoptions. Strange fact: Kaiser announced that the generosity of the Swiss viewers that evening would go towards his new organisation and not to *Terre des Hommes*, with which he had broken ties. And so, while *Terre des Hommes* had organised the huge operation that rescued us the previous day, there was no mention of it at all in the programme. Watching that broadcast was uncomfortable for me, since I couldn't help seeing in it, quite apart from the generosity of the viewers and the power of persuasion of the old humanitarian aid worker, the way that charity towards a certain image of Africa was enacted on Western television screens at the time.

Unlike *Sentinelles*, which did not then develop any direct activities in Rwanda, *Terre des Hommes* had been leading projects in the country since 1991, for children and young people in precarious situations, such as canteens for A.I.D.S. orphans in Kigali, or support for mothers in prisons.

When I interviewed Ariane Zwahlen during the summer of 2020, she told me that she had moved to Rwanda two years before the genocide. She was the only expatriate on the staff and was responsible for around twenty local employees.

Ariane apparently did not see the genocide coming. She talked about the beauty of the landscapes, the gentleness of the people: "What happened seemed like hell suddenly coming into paradise."

She admitted, however, that she knew there was a risk of massacres: "There was tension there, grenades exploding, the *Mille Collines* radio station,[8] it was common knowledge that there were stockpiles of weapons, but at the same time the international community seemed to be mobilised. No-one could imagine it would take on the scope it did."

She told me how she lived through the first days of the genocide. Because she knew the city well, she accompanied the delegates from another organisation who could still move freely around Kigali on April 9, so they could look for a location for a field hospital. There were already roadblocks everywhere, guarded by militiamen and soldiers with bloodshot eyes, and corpses littered the roads. She herself was evacuated the following day.

Once she got home to Switzerland, Ariane participated, from the headquarters in Lausanne, in setting up and implementing an urgent mission, led in parallel by a doctor, Carlos Royo, in the zone controlled by the R.P.F., and by Alexis Briquet in the governmental zone. When she told me Briquet was still alive, I realised that I had supposed him a much older man, already gone.

She suggested putting us in contact.

I accepted with alacrity.

I wrote to Alexis on June 18, 2020. He answered the next day, in a brief e-mail giving me his phone number in France, the country where he was spending part of his retirement. I could not detach my eyes from the screen, where I was very moved to read: *I remember very well a mother and daughter who were able to be evacuated, hidden among the children in the convoy. Might you be that girl, now grown up?*

A first phone call that very evening. He had a low but soft voice, with a slight Swiss accent. I started by thanking him. Twenty-five years after the events.

When Ariane first told me he lived in France, in the same country as me, I was stunned for a few hours, as I became aware of my huge delay. How was it that I had not thought about finding the people who rescued us, when I attached such importance to the necessity to express gratitude, and had been looking for decades for ways to thank those who had supported us?

Why?

Even if *Terre des Hommes* had been a vague, abstract entity for me until then, even if I had no recollection of individual names or faces, shouldn't I have done that? Was it because I thought "they did their work, that's normal"? I do not remember thinking that. I had quite simply not thought about them since then, busy as I was rebuilding my life. And it was only when I talked to Ariane that I became aware that, in fact, there was only a handful of them who were determined to accomplish that incredible feat: getting more than a thousand children out of that country that had become a charnel house. More than a "simple job" by the humanitarian aid workers, it was a huge rescue operation.

So that evening on the telephone, I thanked Alexis Briquet, with a knot in my throat, and also apologised for not doing so earlier. Then I quickly explained my journey since then, the four photographs, the list of children that I wanted to find, so I could show them those images, and tell those children, who were younger than I was at the time, what really happened that day.

Because I remembered the trauma that Fergal Keane still carried when I met him in London in 2009, I thanked Briquet for agreeing to talk to me, to return to those memories that were no doubt painful. He said straight off: "Oh, you know, it's been following me around, under different forms, for a long time now . . ." before adding, "but it is a great pleasure to hear from you."

I understood what he meant without him having to say any more. I had so many questions to ask him about the details of the organisation of the convoys – how on earth did he manage to do all that? He suggested I send them to him by e-mail, and told me, with a slight tinge of fatigue in his voice, that he would try to answer them "even if all this is a long time ago now". He repeated: "It follows me around in different ways, it still follows me, but I do not have the answers for everything." He added that people had often asked him to write his story, that he had started but not finished it.

He appeared to be lucid in considering the past that I brought up to the surface; his words were halting when he admitted that he risked his life back then ... There was a moment of silence on the line, then he concluded: "But it was worth it! I never regretted it for a second. You'd have to be crazy to do it now, but maybe I was crazy then. But it was worth it!"

He talked to me about the couple of Italian journalists who were with him on June 18, then asked me if I remembered a tall blonde woman. At that point, he did not tell me her name. That was Deanna Cavadini, his partner and colleague, who was a delegate from *Terre des Hommes* Italy and had joined him in June, at the same time as the journalists.

It was during that first phone conversation, which lasted almost an hour, that Alexis Briquet told me a few memories of his arrival in Rwanda in April: "When I got there, I did not know what could be done, I did not know anything at all, I had to get up to speed with what was happening, then organise." The idea of the convoys came to him after two or three weeks going back and forth between Burundi and the zone in Rwanda controlled by the genocidal government. "I said to myself, 'If there is any action to take, the one thing to do is to get people out of this mess.'"

He mentioned the support he received from the I.C.R.C. delegate, Philippe Gaillard, to organise the first convoy at the beginning of June, told me he was not surprised that I could not get access to the list of children from *Terre des Hommes*, and suggested I look in the archives of the I.C.R.C. instead.

We agreed to talk again soon, when he had received my questions. He repeated that he remembered me very well, hidden in the truck – "You were the only one with light skin" – and said he remembered that I was smiling then. He delicately enquired after my mother: "Is she still alive?" Yes, she was, but so frail.

I, however, did not ask him anything about his health.

*

The very next day, I sent an e-mail to Alexis with a series of questions about how he organised and succeeded in carrying out the convoys.

He replied that all the questions I was asking would take him on a long journey, which would take many pages to answer in full. He suggested we plan some phone conversations that I could record, while we waited to meet face to face. I also sent him my books in the post. He read them and told me, during our second conversation, that he found them interesting and liked them very much.

On September 2, as I was waiting for a reply from him, and a suggestion for a time to call, he sent me a brief message:

"I've been taking painkillers for a week, for a backache that has sometimes been agonising. I am not used to this. But that's the reason I haven't contacted you. I will call you as soon as there is any significant improvement."

I wished him well, and especially a prompt recovery, the kind of things one says when one doesn't know anything about what the other person is suffering.

He seemed to regain some strength a few days later and took the trouble of connecting me with Mauro, the Italian photographer he had told me about, saying he had taken lots of great pictures of our convoy.

At the beginning of October, we spoke briefly over the telephone: I enquired after his health, and he asked about my progress and encouraged me to keep going. I told him the I.C.R.C. had refused my request for access to the list of children who were looked after following their evacuation by *Terre des Hommes*. In order to have access to it, my name would have to have been on the list. But because I was not officially part of the convoy, my name did not appear anywhere. We spoke again about the possibility of my interviewing him so I could record his memories of 1994.

Then silence again.

The last Saturday in October, at around 8 a.m., he called me.

"I am in the oncology department of Montpellier hospital. I will have to spend some time here to get better. I did not want you to think that I was trying to avoid our interviews. But I need to look after myself, and we can talk about this at a later stage."

It was strange to worry so much about a person I knew so little. And yet, I found myself waiting for my telephone to ring, my heart suspended.

One evening in November, I got a call from Deanna Cavadini, his partner.

Alexis had asked her to contact me. The cancer was aggressive. He had only a few weeks left to live. She told me that he was still conscious sometimes, that I could write to him. This was the first time I had talked to her, and those were the circumstances.

After I hung up, without thinking too much about it, I decided to tell the few other children that I was in contact with, most of whom had left in the last convoy: Annick and Claire, of course, but also Rodrigue, the young man I met in Nice, and then I remembered having read an account of a friend who was a survivor living in Quebec, who said he had found one of his cousins in Burundi after his evacuation from Butare by an N.G.O. I wrote to him too, and he gave me the contact details of that cousin, Angélique, who was then living in Texas. I also wrote to Aristide again, the captain of the Rwandan basketball team, thinking you never know, maybe this time he would answer.

I told them that the man who contributed to our rescue in 1994 was dying, and that, without wanting to put any pressure on anyone, if they wanted to send him a message to tell them that they are now upstanding men and women, and that this was in part because of what he did, then I could give him those messages, so that he might depart this life with his heart brim-full of our rediscovered life stories.

ANNICK "Zouzou" KAYITESI-JOZAN
(convoy of July 3, 1994)

The first one to reply was my friend Annick, nicknamed Zouzou since childhood. She was then living in Uzbekistan with her French husband and their two children. She was one of the first survivors of the genocide to write her story. In her account, titled *Nous existons encore* (We are still alive), published ten years after the genocide, she relates how her mother, her little brother Aimé and her two cousins were killed in Butare on April 30.

Their father and their little sister were already dead, tragically killed by a fire in Belgium. Her sister Aline, who was left for dead in the mass grave where the others were lying, survived and managed to join Annick, with terrible head wounds. Their mother worked at the Karubanda social workers' training school in Butare, the same one where, a few weeks later, the *Terre des Hommes* centre would be established. The day her family was massacred, Annick's life had been spared by the colleague of her mother who had denounced them, so that she could work as a maid for their family. In her harrowing second account, *Même Dieu ne veut pas s'en mêler* (Even God doesn't want to get involved), published in 2017, Zouzou relates how with Aline, whose infected wounds were full of maggots, they had managed to leave the kitchen of that ignominious man to join the last convoy organised by the N.G.O. in the beginning of July:

"At the school – but we now call it the orphanage – a profound silence reigns. We are waiting. One day, a line of buses enters the courtyard. Some of us think our last hour has come, but rumour has it that we are about to be evacuated to Bujumbura, the capital of Burundi. We have no luggage, in a few minutes the school is empty. Nobody hesitates to get on board. The Katyusha rockets whistle over our heads. Very early this morning, one of them fell very close. In the bus, we crouch down when the whistling approaches. The Tutsi from the Rwandan Patriotic Front (R.P.F.) are at the city gates. They are bringing an end to the carnage."

A few weeks later, the two girls arrived in France. Aline was cared for, but would have lifelong after-effects, and the two valiant sisters had to start a new life as survivors and orphans. Zouzou was a brilliant student of political science before later becoming a clinical psychologist. Her life is a very full one, and her immense courage makes her a precious witness who knows how to make past and present chime together and considers how to convey it to our children and the rest of the world.

When I contacted her in November 2020, she sent me a skilfully worded message for Alexis and Deanna, in an e-mail concluding with these words:

"Today, just over a quarter-century later, the pain that was inflicted on us still forces me to invent anew each day that comes. I am happy to be able to put a name to the people who rescued my sister and me, among others. Thank you for not ignoring the children."

*

MANZI CÉDRIC NDAGIJIMANA / RUGIRANGOGA
(convoy of June 5 or 6)

Some of the people who received my call for messages for Alexis in late November 2020 sent audio messages. This was the case of a young man from Lyons to whom Rodrigue had forwarded my e-mail. He was eighteen months old in 1994, and all he knew about his survival was what his older brother and cousins had told him. Like Angélique, he was part of the convoy at the beginning of June.

In the spring of 1994, Manzi was living with his mother, his older brother and older sister in Butare, where his mother was studying to be a nutritionist at Rwanda National University. A cousin was with them for the Easter holidays. Their father was studying in France. His maternal aunt was married to the general director of the Belgian Red Cross in Kigali, whose responsibilities included the Kacyiru orphanage. The uncle and the aunt, along with two of their three children and two nieces staying with them for the holidays, had managed to flee the capital on April 13 along with the boarders and staff of the orphanage, to Butare, where they settled in the buildings of the *Groupe Scolaire*. That is where Manzi and his family joined them on April 20, when the killings had started in the city.

But on April 29 militiamen had invaded the school, obviously with the complicity of some of the employees of the Red Cross, and they had killed Manzi's uncle, aunt and mother – who was carrying him on her back! – along with around forty other people, including children. Manzi's siblings and cousins had survived, guarded by a few adults who, like them, had taken refuge in a school where their lives were under constant threat, especially since the Hutu army had decided to lodge the injured soldiers from Kigali and their families there. After their evacuation to Burundi by *Terre des Hommes*, Manzi's father, who had come home precipitously from France, had come to get them. I discovered on speaking with Manzi that he shared my passion for literature. In 2020 he published his first novel, *La Légende de Havilah*, an Afro-futuristic story inspired by Rwandan mythology.

In his recording for Alexis, Manzi said: "I wanted to add my voice to those of the others to send you a few words, hoping they will stay with you until the end. You did not do this in vain, we are very much alive, and most of us are healthy and full of hope."

In the first days of December, I forwarded the few messages that had arrived, hoping that Alexis would still have a few moments of lucid consciousness to hear them.

He died on December 13, 2020, aged 71. I then realised I was now about the same age as he had been in 1994.

The following summer, I went to meet Deanna in the south of France, where she was spending her holidays with her son and grandchildren. She was an attractive woman with long blond hair. Her skin was tanned and her soft eyes full of goodness. She was finding it hard to get over the sudden death of her partner. She regretted that we had got to know each other so late; she thought that if Alexis had received our messages earlier, it might have helped him to hang on, and he might not have gone so quickly.

For a while I was angry at myself for not starting the journey that led me to them until 2020. But you cannot rewrite the past.

It is not too late, however, to preserve the memory of what Alexis did in 1994, to make it more widely known, and in doing so, to thank this woman in her own lifetime for also contributing to our rescue.

THE CONVOY

*

I took up my research again and did a deep dive into the website of the Residual Mechanism for the International Criminal Tribunal for Rwanda.[9] I asked Deanna whether she could give me copies of the documents she still had from that period, and I recontacted the Italian photographer who was with them.

As the months went by, I managed to reconstitute the events.

I put my initial plan – to give the photographs to the children of the convoy of June 18 – on the back burner. It was at a standstill anyway, since I had not managed to get the list of children either from *Terre des Hommes* or by knocking on the doors of the I.C.R.C. In any case, I wondered, who knows whether that list still exists somewhere?

I also started to think that if I wrote the story of the convoys, and the book was distributed in Rwanda and to the Rwandan diaspora in the wider world, other children might recognise themselves in my story and might possibly contact me.

I needed to recount the facts, to elucidate for myself the questions that Alexis did not have time to answer: what happened? How did he manage to get those hundreds of children out of the country? Who helped him and why? Who was that Costa, who co-signed with him the agreement obtained from the genocidal government? And who were those children, not just their names, but their personal stories? Hutu and Tutsi orphans from before the genocide, like those from the *Groupe Scolaire*, along with those who had seen their parents murdered in April? And the adults, like my mother, how did they manage to be included in the convoys?

In April 1994, Alexis had been a delegate of *Terre des Hommes* for more than fifteen years and was in charge of emergency situations for the Swiss organisation. He came from Geneva, born into a family of the French-speaking upper middle class, and was recruited into the N.G.O. by its founder, Edmond Kaiser. That is where he met his partner, Deanna, who was Swiss-Italian. With her he travelled the world to lead projects supporting children in danger.

He had already been to Rwanda, a short time earlier, on his way back from a mission to neighbouring Burundi, where the N.G.O. also had some projects.

I do not know the exact date, but I think he arrived in Rwanda around April 20, entering via Burundi.

It seems that it was an Italian, a former employee of *Terre des Hommes*, who put him in contact with Pierantonio Costa, a businessman settled in Rwanda for many years who was also the honorary consul for Italy. Costa was evacuated to Burundi with his family at the beginning of the genocide, like the other expatriates, but continued as best he could to go back and forth to Rwanda. For two months he brought help to a large number of people, either by supplying them with money and food, or by participating in rescue operations such as the first convoy of *Terre des Hommes*.

The two men formed an immediate connection. Alexis spoke fluent Italian, and had arrived with concrete means, money and complete freedom of action, without the heavy security procedures of the larger humanitarian agencies. Costa, for his part, knew the country well, and had connections with several Rwandan dignitaries. They would work together for a month and a half, going regularly to Bujumbura before coming back to Rwanda, to attempt to help in any way they could.

To begin with, Alexis's aim was to organise centres where isolated children (orphans, abandoned children, unaccompanied children . . .) could be brought to safety (and be given food and medical care), and then, as soon as possible, to help them cross the border.

During one of his trips to Kigali, Costa made contact with the former secretary of the Union of Rwandan Industrialists, whom he knew well and who was then a member of the interim government. This was the man who would enable them to start negotiating the signature of an agreement between the N.G.O. and the authorities, who in the meantime had fallen back to the south, to Gitarama, because of the fighting between the governmental army and the rebels of the R.P.F. Their presence in that city, located approximately 100 kilometres to the north of Butare, facilitated the two men's progress, because the members of the government were more accessible there.

On May 27, 1994, Alexis and Costa addressed the following letter to the genocidal government, in an attempt to gain their authorisation to launch the large evacuation operation:

Dear Mr President, dear Prime Minister,
We have the honour to submit for your approval a project to assist orphaned children, which was previously discussed with the members of your government, including Minister Defence and Minister Social Affairs [the missing words here show the haste in which the e-mail was no doubt sent] *who also mentioned it to the Prime Minister.*

The positive reception that we found in your government encouraged us to pursue the development of this project, whose principles are as follows: the evacuation to Zaire of 2,000 children now living in orphanages, and the hosting and assistance to as many other unaccompanied children now living in those same orphanages.

We have now reached an agreement in principle with the authorities of Zaire, and with the High Commissioner for Refugees present in Zaire, as well as with the International Red Cross Federation, who are prepared to take on the reception and hosting of the children in Zaire.

Terre des Hommes, *a Swiss N.G.O., with the advice and support of Mr Costa, the Consul for Italy, is ready to take action for the assistance of unaccompanied children on the territory of Rwanda.*

The evacuation mission rests primarily on an air connection between Butare and Bukavu, where the hosting sites have been identified by an official of the International Red Cross Federation. The transportation of the children to be evacuated could only take place by road to Butare, and under the benevolent protection of your law enforcement officers.

We are certain that you are aware of the plight and uncertain future of these children, who, in these tragic hours of the history of your country, number in the thousands. This assistance project also aims to bring international attention to this problem, in expectation of a future time which we hope will be imminent and constructive.

We wish to fully invest in this mission without delay, and with your approval and support, we assure you,

Mr President and Prime Minister, of our respectful and sincere best wishes.

A document three pages long is attached to this letter, presenting the project in greater detail. It mentions the operational centres identified as receiving and hosting the children who could be assisted and evacuated: the centre in Gatagara (a centre for handicapped children run by the Brothers of Charity), the *Groupe Scolaire* in Butare, and the orphanage in Nyanza.

The letter mentions an evacuation by air from Butare to Bukavu. Was Alexis aware at the time that the landing strip of the airport in Butare was not large enough to take planes of the size necessary for the transportation of thousands of children?

As I reread these documents now, knowing what I know about the situation back then, I can see the tightrope those two men must have walked on a daily basis, to gain the approval of the very men who were leading the country to catastrophe. That necessary collaboration.

Alexis and Costa rapidly managed to sign an agreement, as early as May 28, between *Terre des Hommes* and the Rwandan government, represented by the Minister of Labour and Social Affairs, regarding the "Project for assistance to unaccompanied children".

The agreement stipulates: "The Government of Rwanda marks its assent to the proposal presented by the organisation of *Terre des Hommes*, according to the project in the annex, and requests that the following conditions be rigorously applied." There follows a series of six principles. The first stipulates that "all the orphans" will be taken in charge "without any distinction of ethnicity, race or religion", a clause about which the two Westerners must have put up a fight. What it means implicitly is that Tutsi children would in fact be authorised to be included in the evacuation.

During his deposition to the International Criminal Tribunal in 2006, Alexis declared that apart from its necessity in securing the cooperation of the Rwandan authorities, this agreement was indispensable at the time in obtaining support for his evacuation project from other international organisations: the International Committee of the Red Cross and the United Nations if need be.

Alexis and Costa would carry out several rescue operations before they started the convoys, notably at the request of Swiss nationals with family members under threat in Rwanda, or to evacuate employees of international organisations.

Alexis was contacted just before his departure to Rwanda by a Swiss couple who were in the process of adopting a Rwandan orphan girl aged two. These people, having heard on the radio that the N.G.O. was going to send one of its representatives to Rwanda, asked him if he could evacuate the baby.

On his arrival in Rwanda, Alexis managed to get the message to the rural area near Butare where the baby to be adopted was living with her siblings at her grandfather's house. It was the oldest sister, a teenager, who brought her into the city where Alexis picked her up and took her to Burundi. From the ease with which the older sister passed the roadblocks, notably around her village, one may suppose that their parents were Hutu and that she was not threatened by the genocidal militiamen. Once the baby was gone, her big sister would join the other children in the centre managed at the time by *Terre des Hommes* at the Karubanda school in Butare. After the evacuation in July, she would be among those sent to the Bukavu camp in Zaire, where she would stay for two years, until the adoptive grandfather of her sister found her there and brought her to

Switzerland along with the rest of her siblings. The family was extremely grateful to Alexis and remained in contact with him. When the girl grew up she even named her firstborn son after him.

Another remarkable rescue carried out by Costa and Alexis was that of the family of someone called Sunnier in Butare. This Swiss man hosted many members of the family of his Tutsi partner from the very first days of the genocide. The two humanitarian aid workers could only get the couple and their own children across the border, since they had Swiss passports, so they took care of the other children, including Claire and her four sisters, until they could be evacuated later.

Costa and Alexis also carried out a notable support operation for the orphanage at Nyanza, around 40 kilometres to the north of Butare.

When the killings started in the area, the usual boarders at the orphanage managed by Italian priests were joined by a large number of children whose families had been killed and who were seeking refuge with the religious order.

During their first site visit, the two men had found a desperate situation: the reserves of food would soon be exhausted, and the killers were a daily threat outside the walls.

Several evacuation scenarios were considered, even by air, but none of them were feasible.

At the very least, the two men managed to deliver a radio to the orphanage so that the Italian priests could be in communication with their confrères in a community in the province of Padua. Since there was no more electricity available, they had to connect the radio to the battery of their vehicle.

In hindsight, one can imagine how tragic the situation was: the consul, the humanitarian aid worker and the priests spending long minutes trying several frequencies by repeating, "Monselice, do you copy, this is Nyanza, Monselice, please respond!", with the children crowded around them in the dark, their hearts barely beating.

And then the radio started hissing. A voice coming all the way from Italy brought an uncontrollable cry of joy. They all hugged, some were crying. Nyanza was no longer isolated. They were in contact with that little village near Padua, a world away from their reality, but their voices could be heard there despite the threat hanging over them.

At that moment, something infinitesimal yet concrete, a voice in the night, allowed them to imagine that an evacuation might still be possible.

They believed it for a while, then hope faded again.

Their daily life was filled with death. Besides the missionaries there was a doctor, also Italian, who was there trying as best he could to care for those who had taken refuge in the orphanage, after being injured by the militia's machetes. In his memoir, Costa describes him shouting in despair because he had lost a child through the shortage of basic equipment: "You can't lose a child because of a tube costing 50 cents!"

The child had been brought there by his brother, who was barely ten years old, after their parents had been massacred. The killers had broken the little boy's neck, but he was still alive although severely malnourished and dehydrated. He died in Nyanza for the want of a little plastic catheter that would have allowed him to be put on a drip.

After the genocide, the Italian doctor adopted three children from the orphanage and asked Alexis to become their godfather.

Towards the end of the month of May, the fighting between the government troops and the armed forces of the R.P.F. was getting closer to Nyanza. One day when Alexis and Costa were trying to bring food to the orphanage, they came across a crowd of Hutu refugees leaving the township in large family groups. A colonel of the governmental army whom Costa knew had warned them: in a few hours, the road would probably be shut. The two men then decided this might be the time to evacuate the children, when nobody would worry about killing those that look like Tutsi in the confusion.

When they finally reached the orphanage, they found deathly silence. The children were no longer playing: as they listened to the noise of the fighting and the shells close at hand, they were all sitting in silence, immobilised.

In a corner, Father Georges was sitting on a chair, surrounded by five children who had just arrived. The missionary was asking them questions, gently, to find out their story, their names, their ages. Despite the war raging at the door, he made sure to fill in an information card which, if heaven should keep them alive, would allow him to find any surviving family members of these small children, so that the links with their origins, their extended family, would not be broken forever.

Costa and Alexis spent all day trying to find vehicles to carry all the children, in order to make the most of the general disorder to organise an evacuation.

In vain.

When they returned empty-handed to the orphanage, a new terror was waiting for them: the complex was deserted. Everyone had hidden in the basement made of reinforced concrete. There was nothing left to do but wait. They had very little food, a radio and a small stock of medicines. Anything could happen: they could be hit by a shell, liberated by the R.P.F. or attacked by militiamen on the run.

Alexis and Costa left again, driving at walking pace among

a crowd made up of people trying to flee and the routed army, conscious that at any moment an armed soldier could requisition their car. The consul had a very large sum of money in his possession, as he did every time they travelled, to buy food or lives, a fortune that could also sign their death warrant should one of the escapees find it. In order to protect themselves, Costa offered a lift to Butare to the first officer they saw walking in the crowd. In that human river, the car seemed to be floating. It would take them nine hours to travel those 40 kilometres.

The next day they called the orphanage on the radio and Father Georges told them that Nyanza was now safe: the town had been taken by the R.P.F.

In the archives of *Radio Télévision Suisse*, the Swiss public broadcasting service, there is an interview with those same missionaries from the orphanage in Nyanza by a Swiss journalist, filmed a few weeks later, in June. Nothing in the calm voices and smiling faces of those men so much as hints at the anxious times they went through.

From the end of May onwards, Alexis concentrated his activities on Butare, where he was already in contact with another orphanage, one run by the Belgian Red Cross that had found accommodation in the buildings of the largest school in Butare, the *Groupe Scolaire*, after having been evacuated from Kigali. That is where the first convoy would leave from.

First convoys: June 5 and/or 6[10]

Alexis and Costa organised the first convoy(s) to evacuate the children from the orphanage of the Belgian Red Cross in Kacyiru (a neighbourhood of Kigali) to escape the killings and the fighting taking place in the capital. They had found refuge in Butare from April 13 onwards. The group included several hundred children, along with carers and their families. They had settled in the *Groupe Scolaire*, an institution founded in the colonial era and comprised of a primary and secondary school, whose buildings were empty at the time because the students were all on Easter holidays.

In the following days, a large number of Tutsi, fleeing the massacres and hoping to find help with the Red Cross, had come to find shelter there.

They were attacked in the *Groupe Scolaire* on April 29 by the Hutu military and militia. According to eyewitness accounts, 27 children and 22 adults were killed there. At least 700 children were in the complex and their survival was all the more precarious because wounded soldiers from the governmental army had just been transferred there from Kigali airport.

The cohabitation between the children and the soldiers was untenable.

After the signature of the agreement with the government, Alexis had contacted other organisations who might be able to assist with the evacuation.

The I.C.R.C. based in Burundi had agreed to supply the vehicles and to take charge of all of the children whom *Terre des*

Hommes could manage to get out of the country. On June 4 at Bujumbura, the delegate of the I.C.R.C. informed Costa that the operation was planned for the following day. He invited Costa to accompany him to Butare. Alexis was spending the night in Rwanda to take care of the last preparations. During a previous trip, Alexis and Costa had been in contact with the *préfet* of Butare, Sylvain Nsabimana, who, on the basis of the agreement signed with the minister, had undertaken to help them complete the evacuation.

In the agreement, in fact, the Rwandan government had committed to "assist *Terre des Hommes* by all possible means, in particular by putting transportation at their disposal in order to assemble the convoys as part of the evacuation operation, and provide the resources necessary for the security and protection of the children and other persons taking part in the programme".

A colonel from the governmental army, François Munyengango, a liaison officer for the I.C.R.C. charged with this function by the Ministry of Defence, was responsible for the security of the operation that day.

On June 5 at 9 a.m., Costa and Daniel Philippin, a delegate of the I.C.R.C., were already at the border between Rwanda and Burundi with cars and trucks, waiting for a sign from Alexis confirming that all the arrangements had been made for the children to leave Rwanda. The two of them were supposed to go to Butare with the vehicles. That is when they received a radio call from Bujumbura informing them that the I.C.R.C. headquarters in Geneva was refusing to authorise the operation. According to Costa's memoir, Daniel Philippin then screamed into the radio: "What do you mean: the operation is not authorised? Do you realise we are already at the border and that

Alexis already has everything prepared?" But the order was irrevocable: the men and resources of the I.C.R.C. could not be deployed beyond the border.

Costa left Philippin at the border and went into Rwanda alone to join Alexis in Butare. They then decided to give it their all.

They needed to obtain assurance that a few of the authorities would protect the convoy, and also to find the vehicles required to transport several hundred children.

After a few back-and-forth trips in the city, the two men managed to find Sylvain Nsabimana.

As for the cars or trucks, contrary to what had been stated in the agreement signed on May 28, the government had made no vehicles available to the organisation, who would therefore be obliged to rent them at a very high price, and for all of the convoys. It was a highly colourful character, the Yugoslav priest Vjekoslav Ćurić, nicknamed Vjeko, who would help Alexis and Costa find those vehicles.

Vjeko was a Franciscan friar originally from Bosnia who had refused to be evacuated from his parish in Kivumu at the beginning of the genocide. He had set himself the task of driving across the border from Burundi in trucks loaded with food and medical supplies to help people in hiding and the religious orders in the south of the country, sometimes returning to Burundi with Tutsi hidden in the trucks.

Alexis had met Vjeko when he first arrived in Bujumbura. The relations between the priest and the humanitarian aid worker, who had just spent a year in Bosnia on a mission with *Terre des Hommes*, were cordial. Vjeko spoke Kinyarwanda and knew how to negotiate with the militiamen at the many roadblocks in their path.

*

That day, in the early afternoon, it was thanks to Vjeko's contacts that Alexis and Costa were able to find a few minibuses the children and their escorts from the Red Cross piled into as best they could, ready to go.

But they were not the only ones to board the minibuses. A few Tutsi adults who had been hiding in the *Groupe Scolaire* managed to slip among them into the vehicles. In that country, where, in parallel with the genocide, a war was raging whose outcome was anything but certain, a few soldiers who were at the school, and who had probably themselves participated in the massacres of Tutsi, demanded that their own children be taken to Burundi. They certainly wanted to get them away from the violence. It was an absurd situation where the genocidal soldiers thus allowed a few of the victims they had not been able to kill to leave, so long as the rescuers also took their own offspring.

This scene contains all the ambiguity which the humanitarian aid workers had to come to terms with, this collaboration with the killers to save the children.

However, as the vehicles were leaving the *Groupe Scolaire*, a horde of militiamen, informed about the preparations for departure, had crowded before the front gates to stop them from leaving.

Only the arrival of the *préfet* and long minutes of negotiations with him and Colonel François Munyengango would at last allow the convoy to depart. At 5 p.m.

The *préfet* and the colonel led the procession in the former's car; Alexis and Costa were in the last vehicle. The consul had come from Burundi with his pockets full of banknotes and was constantly handing them out to the militiamen in order to buy their safe passage.

At each roadblock, the same anxious waiting. The militiamen

climbed up on the vehicles shouting: "There are heaps of Tutsi in here!" Several times, Colonel Munyengango threatened them with his gun to make them back off. It took more than six hours to travel the 30 kilometres to the border.

Once they got there, everyone had to get out of the vehicles to cross on foot the no-man's-land between the two countries to get to the vehicles of the I.C.R.C. waiting on the Burundi side. The Tutsi adults who had managed to board the vehicles in Butare, some of whom were seriously injured, were not authorised to leave Rwanda. The Rwandan authorities took as a pretext that their names did not appear on the list of children and escorts that had been previously drawn up. They were thus sent back to Butare.

Claire and her sisters, the nieces of the Sunniers, were part of this group. Any return to the *Groupe Scolaire* was unthinkable, for they would have been massacred there. Alexis then obtained as an emergency measure from the nuns running the Karubanda school in Butare that they make their buildings available to *Terre des Hommes* so those who were turned back at the border and the other children who had stayed at the *Groupe Scolaire* could be safely housed there.

It was from the Karubanda school that the second and third convoy would depart.

After crossing the border, the children of the first convoy were taken care of by the Red Cross. For security reasons, the decision was made to stop at a refugee camp run by the organisation near the border, in Kayanza, rather than driving to the capital in the middle of the night.

*

The story of that night spent in Kayanza was told to me by a strange character, undoubtedly the most unusual of all the people that this investigation led me to encounter.

This is how I met him.

In June 2021, I was invited to speak about the history of the *Terre des Hommes* convoys by the Holocaust museum in Paris, the *Mémorial de la Shoah*, and the Ibuka France organisation, along with other survivors who had been saved by actions of rare humanity. The session was filmed and broadcast on the website of the Mémorial.

A few days later, I received a message from Jacques Morel, whose website I have already mentioned as a veritable goldmine of archives about the genocide against the Tutsi.

He had watched my presentation online. He told me he had a list of the children evacuated by *Terre des Hommes* in the beginning of June, and that not only could he send it to me by e-mail, but he could also put me in touch with Michel Seine,[11] the man who had given it to him. Seine was formerly with the International Federation of Red Cross and Red Crescent Societies, who were in charge of that refugee camp in Kayanza, in the north of Burundi. Seine told Morel that he had received two convoys of children coming from an orphanage in Kigali, at night.

Aged 86, Seine lived in the outskirts of Rouen. When Morel gave me his telephone number, he informed me that before working for the Red Cross, Seine had been in the military. He also warned me that Seine sometimes spoke rather incoherently.

Over the phone, Michel Seine told me several different stories that seemed to me to be unconnected. He told me he had photographs and numerous archival documents related to the convoys, which he could make available to me. I decided to pay him a visit, in the company of my husband.

The old gentleman who greeted us in front of the building of his council flat and led us into his home seemed to be in good shape. He had us sit down in a living room filled with knick-knacks of all shapes and sizes, of which several obviously came from the African continent. And then he started talking.

We spent four hours listening to him.

Four interminable hours of him essentially telling us the story of his life, and particularly his experience during the war in Algeria. This was an isolated man living in the past. I found his verbal diarrhoea intolerable. He went off on a thousand and one tangents and told us every detail of his story: his military service in Oran, his numerous missions up to 1962, notably for the Specialised Administrative Sections. On his return from Algeria, he had a series of professional and personal problems. It was Africa that put him back in the saddle, thanks to a first mission with the Red Cross, who sent him to Senegal in 1984, with no training, first as an accountant, then as a programme director. After that he went to Mali, to Congo-Brazzaville, to Chad and Central Africa, after being recruited by a large French business group. Then to other countries for various missions in which he boasted of having done great work each time, despite his initial lack of training and experience.

The underlying story he was telling here was the familiar tale of how a band of adventurers were able to gain the kind of status and positions in Africa they could never have aspired to at home, merely because of their nationality.

After three hours spent listening to the account of his missions in Algeria, I began to grow impatient: I had come to seek traces of the *Terre des Hommes* convoys, not to listen to this man's fixed ideas and nostalgia for colonial times.

Luckily my husband was with me! He kept throwing glances at me saying, "Patience, can't you tell there's no use trying to rush him?" Michel Seine finally asked Yann to follow him into the kitchen where he kept his Rwandan files hidden. We realised that he entertained strange theories, that he had written to various people in high office, notably to the successive French presidents, with numerous attempts at contact, and that he sometimes even made claims with the post office to be sure that his letters were being properly delivered.

In 1994, Seine was in Rwanda from February onwards, in charge of logistics for the Red Cross. When the genocide started, he happened to be near the border with Zaire and was evacuated, before going on to Burundi. From there, he was given the task of setting up a refugee camp for the Tutsi living close to the border who had managed to flee.

He finally talked to us about *Terre des Hommes* in highly critical terms. He accused the N.G.O. of organising the evacuation poorly, of letting adults get into the trucks that were meant to transport only children. When I asked him whether it was better to leave people to be massacred, it was probably the military man in him who replied that orders were orders and that one should never contravene an agreement made with the authorities.

In the end we did not learn much in Rouen. A few weeks later, Seine sent me the entirety of his Rwandan archive through the post, saying that he wished to close the door on that part of his life once and for all.

The lists of children he sent me left me at a loss rather than shedding any light.

There were in fact three lists, titled "Orphans and escorts from Rwanda departing for Bukavu (Zaire)". According to these documents, there was a first convoy that set off for Zaire on June 8, which seems to agree with the date of the first *Terre des Hommes* convoy of June 5. That group was made up of 295 people, of which sixteen were adult escorts, 136 orphans from Kigali (Red Cross), 119 other children (probably the Tutsi survivors who had taken refuge in the *Groupe Scolaire*) and "24 members of three families". One of these three families bears the name of Colonel François Munyengango – I assume he also made the most of the opportunity of this evacuation to get his own family to safety.

What I also noticed was that, contrary to the initial decision to evacuate only children under the age of twelve, around 20 per cent of the refugees were older than that.

All of this must have contributed to the irritation of our military man redeployed as an aid worker, who could not abide that orders be disobeyed.

The second list identified a group of 291 people who left for Bukavu on June 14. Who were these people? Was it an additional convoy? I remembered that during his deposition to the I.C.T.R. in 2006, Alexis was asked to confirm the number of convoys that were organised by *Terre des Hommes*. It seems that in a previous session he had mentioned four convoys, including two organised on June 5, then 6. But in 2006, he said that was a mistake and that there were only three of them. This list puzzled me. The group included a larger proportion of escorts (38) and this time children over twelve years made up more than half of it.

Alexis is no longer here to throw light on this.

What is certain is that after that convoy (or those first two) in the beginning of June, the I.C.R.C. and the Red Cross decided to withdraw their support for the evacuations organised by *Terre des Hommes*.

Costa, for his part, under pressure from his family, who did not want him to take any more risks, stopped accompanying Alexis from that day onwards.

He returned to Rwanda after the genocide, where he was officially recognised as *"umurinzi w'igihango"*, the equivalent of Righteous among the Nations.

Costa's rescue activities during the genocide were widely recognised and received media attention, contrary to those of Alexis, notably in Italy (where he was made *Commendatore Ordinis Sancti Gregorii Magni*, then *Commendatore Ordine al Merito della Repubblica Italiana*) and in Belgium (where he was made *Chevalier de l'Ordre de la Couronne de Belgique*).

A documentary film was made about his story, which came out in 2004, along with the account I mentioned earlier, both titled *La Lista del Console* (The consul's list).

Pierantonio Costa died in early January 2021, twenty days after Alexis Briquet.

June 1994. After Costa's withdrawal, Alexis would not be alone for long. The delegate from *Terre des Hommes* Italy, Deanna Cavadini, joined him on June 9 in Bujumbura. She arrived with an Italian couple, the journalist Patrizia Miazzo and the photographer Mauro Parmesani, who were tasked with documenting the rescues as they happened for the Swiss and Italian public and for the N.G.O.'s donors.

Those donors had given enough to fill a plane with eleven tonnes of clothing, medical supplies and food, which Deanna brought with her. Two nurses were with them, charged with the task of sending any severely wounded children who needed surgery to an Italian hospital.

The plane returned empty to Italy, transporting only the little orphan girl to her Swiss adoptive family, along with the two nurses.

The Karubanda school in Butare became the new operational centre for *Terre des Hommes* in the southern zone of Rwanda. Briquet employed what remained of the team from the Red Cross orphanage in Kigali to look after the children day to day, while the humanitarian aid workers continued to go back and forth to Bujumbura. From then onwards, the Hutu residents who were hiding Tutsi children, and the kind souls who found little survivors after the massacres in the hills, brought them to the school. It seems Alexis obtained an agreement from the *préfet* and the colonel that a few trusted military men should provide a modicum of security around the institution, keeping the militiamen at bay.

That is where my mother and I found shelter on June 8.

Second convoy: June 18

During my first telephone call with Alexis, he said that our convoy had been the easiest one to organise. He had used the same terms fourteen years earlier in his statement to the International Criminal Tribunal. The easiest one.

The I.C.R.C. and the Red Cross having withdrawn their support from *Terre des Hommes*, Alexis and Deanna had to manage on their own to find trucks, always thanks to the help of Friar Vjeko.

In order to avoid the difficulties presented during the previous convoy, the two humanitarian aid workers, assisted by some Rwandan employees at the centre, paid particular attention to the composition of the lists of children to be evacuated: none of them could be older than twelve, as agreed with the authorities.

During his deposition to the International Criminal Tribunal, Alexis confirmed that the framework had been respected that time. He did not mention the presence of an adult – my mother – and her teenage daughter.

He told the judges of the second sitting of the Tribunal that, on the morning of the evacuation, a crew from the B.B.C. had arrived and asked if it could accompany the convoy. Briquet said that he was reluctant. He was afraid that their presence would constitute an additional risk. He finally accepted, but insisted on the fact that they must be as discreet as possible, and not film at the roadblocks when the militiamen were aggressive.

The children boarded the trucks calmly. I could see in the photographs how all of them were well dressed, thanks to the clothing brought from Italy by Deanna. Each one wore a label, with their name and a number, stapled to their top. The journalists filmed the preparations for departure. At the Tribunal, two videos were shown and Alexis was asked to comment on them. I was not granted access to those documents. All that I have is the documentary from the B.B.C. "Panorama" programme that Fergal Keane gave me. The convoy on June 18 only takes up two minutes of it. You can see, in the courtyard of the Karubanda school, the doors of one of the trucks being partially closed, held with a rope to let some air into the container where around 50 children are sitting, under the attentive eyes of Deanna and the *préfet*.

Then come a few images evidently discreetly filmed from within the truck while the vehicles are moving, passing the roadblocks at which you can clearly see the weapons of the militiamen: machetes, sickles, plain sticks or clubs. They seem idle, watch the trucks move through, while a voice-over says that the *préfet* has conducted acrimonious negotiations to enable their passage. His black sedan goes ahead of the trucks to be the first to approach the killers. The journalists were able to film close-up shots of the children's faces inside the trucks; one has a huge bandage on the top of his head, another is asleep, his little body rocked by the movement of the vehicle.

And finally the images filmed at the border, a shot of Alexis lifting up a little child to get him out of the truck.

The camera shows groups of children leaving for the border, while an interview with the *préfet* begins.

I found a complete transcription of this interview on the france-genocidetutsi.org website, apparently taken from the exhibits in the I.C.T.R. trial, and bearing the number Exhibit D 460 b. At times it is surreal. As I read it, I thought that what the *préfet* Nsabimana said sounded like Eichmann, the Nazi official, but a reversed Eichmann, who might have argued that he was only obeying orders to save lives. I do not know whether Nsabimana was trying to offload responsibility for the rescue by presenting himself as an official who was simply obeying orders, because he knew he was being observed by the genocidal soldiers present at the border post, by Colonel Nteziryayo who would soon replace him in his position, or whether what he was saying genuinely reflected his thoughts.

When the journalist asks him why he agreed to help the humanitarian aid workers to evacuate the children, this is what Nsabimana says:

"Um . . . I am here to help the children . . . cross the border in accordance with . . . an agreement signed between the Rwandan government and *Terre des Hommes*. [. . .]

". . . because I am obliged to accompany them to see that they really cross the border and I am responsible for these children. So I have to know whether they have left or not. If there are any problems, I have to solve them. [. . .]"

Later on he declares:

". . . helping children is part of my work, it's part of my work. I am obliged to, I am in authority. I must act as an authority, as someone who responds to orders given higher up, and when I receive orders from higher up, I follow them. So I can't not want to, I can't not help them, because I am obliged to. So it's all part of . . . it's all in order, it's justice, and the normal way of things."

Only part of this response is shown in the B.B.C. documentary.

The rest of the interview is perhaps on a tape somewhere in the archives of the B.B.C., and certainly on a shelf in the

International Criminal Tribunal who were able to transcribe what Sylvain Nsabimana said, but I was not able to find it on the website of the International Residual Mechanism for Criminal Tribunals in Rwanda and ex-Yugoslavia. And it is also one of the rare pieces of written evidence I own that I was there on the border on June 18, 1994, because we are in fact mentioned in it.

The B.B.C. journalist asks the *préfet* who can and cannot cross the border from Rwanda. Nsabimana offers a convoluted response, full of equivocal phrases, for there is no question of his admitting that Tutsi are no longer allowed to leave the country.

Question: "Adults probably would not [[inaudible]] to travel to the [[inaudible]]?"

Answer by SN: "Hmm . . . I do not think so. If they have . . . if they have documentation, papers, they can cross. If they are in order, they can, and if they are not in order [[inaudible]]. At every roadblock, um, they must . . . there is a minimum of documentation that they must show, and notably either an I.D. card, or a paper allowing you to cross, a *laissez-passer*, or a passport for a foreigner or a Rwandan who wishes to leave. We let people leave, those who want to leave can do so as long as they have the right documents. Um, at the roadblocks, I am not always there to see what's going on at all the roadblocks. What I do know is that we gave the order to let whoever wants to pass go through, whoever wants to leave. But when they are stopped and then taken away, we can see why, um, what the . . . what the problem was. Then we consider in the moment when it's O.K. We tell the roadblock that the guy should get through and he does get through. But it can happen that the guy doesn't get through because he doesn't have them all. So his documents are not in order. In that case, I do not know how to answer especially since I was not there, but in a particular case, then I give an answer." And so on and so forth, for a few more sentences.

The journalist insists, he wants to know what happens when someone has an I.D. showing they are Tutsi.

"Why not? Why not? Um . . . I can give you an example: I in fact . . . I have these children here. I do not even know if these children are Hutu or Tutsi. It's not my problem, in fact."

He talks about Tutsi nuns, about the Bishop of Butare who is Tutsi, and says: "We are protecting them so they are not disturbed." And he continues trying to prove that the only problem is connected to the fact that people do not always have the right papers.

And as he rambles on, he adds this:

". . . there is a lady and her child. A lady who is Tutsi I think and who has . . . who is French and has just gone through here. I have just said that we have nothing to do with [[inaudible]] for everything. She can go through. So therefore, it's not because you are Tutsi or Hutu that you can go through the roadblocks automatically. So there is a minimum of documents that you need for the roadblocks, and if you have them, whether you're Hutu or Tutsi, you get through. But if you do not have them, whether you're Hutu or Tutsi, you won't get through."

After reading the transcription of Nsabimana's interview, I wanted to have another look at the passport my mother presented at the border guards' counter that day, as if to convince myself that it did exist. There was a big drawer in my wardrobe where I kept the photographs, notebooks and various papers from the past all mixed together. I rarely opened it so as not to be tempted to dive into it completely.

The passport was there. It seemed almost new. I looked at my mother's photograph, she is still so young, with that afro

I remember her wearing until 1994. Then I turned the page.

I was astonished to discover that it was in fact stamped by the Rwandan border guard on June 18, 1994. And that their colleagues in Burundi also did so in turn, a few metres away, affixing the official stamps. And so, in the middle of the genocide, when more than 800,000 people had already been killed, when people were still being massacred a few metres away from us, that masquerade took place. My mother paid for the stamps, and we left the country in the most official possible way. An unimaginable exception.

When I spoke to Alexis Briquet over the telephone for the first time, I asked him how it came about that he had accepted us into the convoy reserved for children. He told me: "It was the *préfet* who asked me to do it. Someone had interceded on your behalf with him, some nuns, I believe."

I think it was Sister Christine and her colleagues.

Third convoy: July 3

During the last two weeks of June, the centre managed by *Terre des Hommes* in Butare took charge of a large number of other children, notably around 60 of them who had been taken out of a town called Kaduha, in a prefecture neighbouring Gikongoro.

The story of the children from Kaduha was told to me by my friend the historian Hélène Dumas, with whom I regularly discussed my investigation.

During her own research she had found a large number of documents left by a German nun, Sister Milgitha Kösser, who had been living in the Euthymia convent in Kaduha for more than two decades. In 1994, she was managing the health centre, next to the church, with another nun, Sister Quirina.

The two women had tried to help tens of thousands of Tutsi who had sought refuge in the parish of Kaduha. But on April 21 the Hutu had started massacring them. It was only after two days, once the Hutu had left, that the two nuns had been able to leave their house to look for survivors. Sister Milgitha, as well as rescuing them, had wanted to document what had happened. She had taken many photographs, rare documentary evidence in that time and place of the extermination that was being carried out with no outside witnesses.

The nuns would keep dozens of children who had escaped the April killings in their convent, facing daily harassment from the militiamen, whom Milgitha managed to appease for a time by giving them all the money in her possession.

As well as the photographs, she would preserve all the

written evidence of that extreme period. In 2016, shortly before her death, Milgitha gave the file containing her archives to the executive secretary of the National Commission for the Fight against Genocide. For their records.

It was in reading through that file that Hélène Dumas found clues that might be of interest to me and had the kindness to send me a copy.

On 15 June, under pressure from the genocidal *sous-préfet* of Kaduha, the nuns had finally agreed to leave Rwanda.

Milgitha and the other nun were obliged to leave behind the surviving children and wounded adults, a total of 85 people. They had taken the trouble beforehand of placing them in the care of the few Hutu employees of the health centre, a doctor and a nurse, who had not joined those conducting the genocide.

In the Kaduha archives, we found a hand-written document, a simple sheet of lined paper making note of the transfer of the surviving children to *Terre des Hommes*, a transfer that must have been negotiated by the nun with the humanitarian aid workers before her departure. Dated June 23, 1994, it says: "The *Terre des Hommes* Foundation is in possession of 60 children, orphans initially taken in charge by Sister Milgitha Kösser at the health centre in Kaduha."

The paper was signed by the Rwandan director of the centre in Butare (a former employee of the Red Cross) and the nurse in charge of the health centre of Kaduha. Those children would be part of the last convoy to Burundi, the one on July 3, 1994.

That evacuation took place in conditions that were totally different from ours.

At the beginning of July, the war was getting closer to Butare. The Hutu governmental army was losing the fight against the

Rwandan Patriotic Front, which was composed mostly of Tutsi exiles and by then controlled most of the country.

On June 22, France had decided to launch the military-humanitarian *Opération Turquoise*, ostensibly to come to the aid of the victims. At that time, however, the vast majority of Tutsi were already dead. The operation was authorised by the United Nations Security Council. But the vote included numerous abstentions, for many members, knowing the connivance of the French government with the genocidal regime, feared that the intervention would mostly serve to support the Hutu army.

Opération Turquoise was deployed from Goma and Bukavu, two cities in Zaire on the western border with Rwanda, and would establish, from early July onwards, what was called a "humanitarian safety zone" on the 20 per cent of the territory of Rwanda that had not yet been liberated by the R.P.F. Hundreds of thousands of Hutu would be received there, civilians, militiamen and still-armed soldiers fleeing the advance of the Tutsi army whose vengeance they feared. Most of them would finish their journey in Zaire, where they would join the vast numbers of their countrymen in huge refugee camps, still under the control of the genocidal government.

But at the time, on July 2, the noise of mortar shells and gunshots could still be heard throughout the hills around Butare, very close to the centre where *Terre des Hommes* still had responsibility for roughly 600 children.

I found few archives about the last convoy, which was carried out in great haste. On July 2, the Rwandan director of the centre had sent a call for help to Alexis Briquet, who was in Burundi at the time. The two humanitarian aid workers, Alexis and Deanna, again accompanied by the Italian journalists, immediately came to Butare.

During our telephone conversation, Alexis told me how, as soon as he arrived in Butare, he went to ask for help from the French military who were part of *Turquoise* and based not far from there. They were the ones who requisitioned buses and fuel from the authorities. The mayor had protested, but the French forces were in conquered territory and a squadron of the special force thus escorted the convoy to the border.

Just as with the other convoys, the buses had to stay in Rwanda. Alexis had managed to mobilise several dozen private vehicles from Bujumbura, cars, vans, buses, to come to meet them at the border, by broadcasting a radio appeal from Butare.

According to eyewitness accounts, the evacuation took place in a somewhat chaotic fashion. The Hutu in Butare were also fleeing the fighting, both the killers and the innocent, along with their families, and the authorities too . . . Most of them were heading towards the zone controlled by the French army in the west of the country, but some of them, like the *préfet* Nsabimana and his family, decided to go to Burundi, blending into the *Terre des Hommes* convoy.

Terre des Hommes had organised a reception centre in a disused depot in Bujumbura in mid-June. That is where the 600 children who arrived on July 3 were taken. Some of them were picked up by family members who were already refugees in Burundi. The others were sent to Zaire, as part of an operation conducted by the I.C.R.C.

Of the thousand children who were evacuated in June and July – according to the final reports of the N.G.O. – 554 went to the refugee camp in Bukavu in Zaire, where they were taken into the care of the Belgian Red Cross, 222 were taken in by families in Burundi, and 262 stayed in the *Terre des Hommes* reception centre in Bujumbura.

This last group was repatriated to Rwanda a few months later, into new centres the N.G.O. had established in Butare.

In December 1995, *Terre des Hommes* was one of the 44 N.G.O.s that the Rwandan post-genocide government had asked to leave the country. This was a rare occurrence in the history of humanitarian operations in Africa: the new regime, set up by the R.P.F. – which had put an end to the genocide of the Tutsi and of the few non-extremist Hutu politicians who survived the massacres – decided to expel a large number of humanitarian organisations whose work was deemed to be unnecessary or whose political stance was unwelcome.

Those were troubled times, the country was bled dry, and the differences between the standard of living of the expatriates and the locals set people's teeth on edge. Some could not hide their resentment of the Westerners who had abandoned the country during the genocide while at the same time deploying vast resources in aid of the Hutu refugees in the camps in Congo.

What exactly was held against *Terre des Hommes*? As far as I know, what was remembered of that last convoy in early July 1994 was that it was organised with the French soldiers from the *Turquoise* military-humanitarian operation, and that it enabled the exfiltration of *préfet* Nsabimana and his family. The management of the children's centre in Bujumbura was also considered insufficiently rigorous, a few children having been adopted by families in Burundi and never returned. Moreover, I imagine that one of the more recent projects of the N.G.O., which consisted of supporting minors accused of genocide and was partly managed by French employees with little experience, was not to everyone's liking.

*

The teams of expatriates from the Lausanne organisation left the country, placing their operations in the care of Rwandan organisations, or of foreign ones allowed to remain. A chapter thus closed in sadness and no doubt this bittersweet ending explains why the happy events – our rescue during the genocide – would gradually be forgotten, or at least would not be given the recognition it deserved in the following decades.

Finally, I now understand that the fact that Alexis was a witness for the defence of the *préfet* Nsabimana, when he was judged at the International Criminal Tribunal in Arusha, may have shocked some survivors.

I do not wish to dwell any further on those events. Whatever lack of understanding he had about the political situation in the country, whatever his mistakes may have been, you cannot take away the fact that Alexis showed immense courage and generous humanity, and that with the help of only a handful of people he rescued several hundred Tutsi, where others had cravenly abandoned us to our fate.

Alexis has died and is no longer here to answer all the questions I still wish to ask him.

How did he feel about it all? Why was there an age limit of twelve for the children to be evacuated? Who had made that decision? Who is that man with Asian features who appears in several photographs of the convoy on June 18, from the time of departure from Butare onwards? Keane says in his book that it was a Japanese aid worker. Deanna and Mauro do not remember his name.

And then there are other, more complex questions, which I dearly wish I could have discussed with him. For example, why did the *préfet* Nsabimana and Colonel Munyengango agree to help him rescue us? Someone told me that the officer knew he was infected with a virus that was incurable at the time, and people had interpreted his bravery as a way of leaving behind a good deed before he died. Did he believe in paradise?

As for Nsabimana, he symbolises on his own the ambiguities of so many Hutu during the genocide.

He was arrested in Kenya, where he had taken refuge after the fall of the Hutu regime. In 2006, he appeared for the first time before the International Criminal Tribunal for Rwanda at Arusha in Tanzania. For his defence, he called on the Irish reporter and the Swiss humanitarian aid worker, asking them to come and give evidence that he had saved Tutsi children.

I spent long hours reading the depositions of the two men to the second sitting of the Tribunal. Both of them were called to give evidence during two or three days in 2006, one month apart.

The Nsabimana file was part of the long trial which was known as that of the "Butare Six". It was of six public authorities who were considered the principal organisers of the massacres in the prefecture. These were:

– Pauline Nyiramasuhuko, the Minister of Families and the Advancement of Women of the interim government, and her son Arsène Shalom Ntahobari, respectively the wife and son of the rector of the university;

– Joseph Kanyabashi, the mayor of Butare;

– Élie Ndayambaje, the former mayor of the town of Kibayi, close to the border, in fact the very town where my mother's family lived;

– Sylvain Nsabimana, the *préfet* of Butare;

– Alphonse Nteziryayo, the officer who would replace him at his post on June 19. He was also originally from the same area as my mother.

*

Looking through the archives on the website of the Residual Mechanism of the International Criminal Tribunals was particularly trying. I was only able to find two videos taken from the rushes of the B.B.C. Additionally, reading the depositions of Alexis Briquet and Fergal Keane led me to discover the arcane language and incomprehensible procedures of the hearings. How many survivors have been able to access the trials of those who organised the genocide of their families? How many were able to understand them? There is information in those archives that is important for us all, but it is buried in pages and pages of procedural convolutions and in legal jargon which is unintelligible to the uninitiated. How can these be made more accessible to the victims? Has anyone even considered this issue?

In June 2011, Nsabimana was sentenced to 25 years in prison for his role in the genocide of the Tutsi in Butare. The International Criminal Tribunal found him guilty of dereliction of his legal duty, as a *préfet*, of protecting the vulnerable people for whom he was responsible in his jurisdiction (notably the Tutsi who had taken refuge in front of his office at the prefecture). He was therefore considered an accomplice in the genocide, but it could not be established that he had been the direct agent of a massacre or a murder, or carried out any active and public incitation to genocide.

I also found out recently that, contrary to what I had first thought, the *préfet* already knew of the decision of his superiors to remove him from his role when he accompanied our convoy on June 18. Why did he help us? Was it a way, like Colonel Munyengango's, of leaving a positive trace, when he knew he had been dismissed?

The prosecutor of the I.C.T.R. declared on the subject of the "Butare Six" that the genocide would not have been possible in

Butare without the participation of these figures of authority. All of them appealed the verdict. The appeal judgement, pronounced in December 2015, marked the permanent closure of the tribunal. All of the sentences of those found guilty were later revised downwards.

The appeal tribunal, presided over by the Italian judge Fausto Pocar, justified this reduction in their sentences with the "harm" caused to those six people by a verdict arrived at ten years after their incarceration.

This trial was considered the costliest and longest in international criminal justice.

The former *préfet* Nsabimana thus found his freedom again, his sentence having been reduced to eighteen years in prison, in other words, exactly the length of time that he had already served.

During my research, I realised with astonishment that most of the men sentenced by the I.C.T.R. in Arusha for having been the organisers of the genocide were now free, their sentences having been reduced after an appeal, or for "good behaviour"...

None of those on trial for genocide in Butare had pleaded guilty or expressed any remorse, much less apologised to the victims.

Today I know that the killers are of no interest to me. I wish to devote all my energy to the story of the victims, to speak about our tribulations, the trauma from which we cannot heal, but also about our delicate solidarity.

In the summer of 2022, when I started writing this account, I got a telephone call from Hélène Dumas. She told me about a visit she made to some survivors of Kaduha, during which a woman had told her that her little sister was one of those children evacuated to Bujumbura by *Terre des Hommes*. She had never come home, but lived with a family in Burundi, then got married and still lived there. Both sisters had thought the other was long since dead. Now they had found each other again and talked regularly over the telephone. Hélène and I agreed that she should give me the young woman's contact information, so that I could send her the photographs I had found. Who knew? Maybe she would recognise herself on one of them?

That day, as I finished the conversation, I thought about the principle mentioned by Daniel Mendelsohn, at the end of his book *Three Rings*, a principle according to which there is a real connection between all things, and I realised that if it has taken me thirty years to write this story, it is because life needed time to interlace the fine friendships and encounters required for its root system to spread and flourish.

4
Our Time Has Come

"I cannot find consolation by saying to myself, 'Yes, I am harming this man by being only this cold lens when he, this man, needs a little brotherhood at a terrible time.' I cannot say to myself, 'Yes, I am harming this man, but I am allowing other people to become aware . . .' That is not enough. And in the case of Rwanda, the harm was done. What use was it to take photographs? For history? I cannot see the point. And for whose history? Who are they intended for, our photographs? They are intended for Europe and the United States, and that represents what percentage of the total of humanity? There is nothing universal about us, we are the products of a certain culture, and we devise our production for a certain culture, for a certain society."

Extract from an interview of Luc Delahaye in the documentary film "The War Reporter", directed by Patrick Chauvel and Antoine Novat, 1998

I had planned to tell the story of the convoys. At least that was my only objective when I decided to write, in 2020, after the death of Alexis Briquet. But the pathway I then took to find all the elements required to write this story, the memories of some, the archives of others, led me to ask and seek answers for unexpected questions.

With each door that closed, with each disappointment at a lead turning into a dead end, against all expectations, I learned a lot. Not only about the chronology of our rescue, but also about the way that history, the whole story of the genocide, had been told throughout the world by pictures taken by foreigners whose narrative ended up being imposed on us all.

I spent long hours examining the pictures, hoping to find my face in them, then also those of the other children I met during my investigation. And when I could find nothing of us, I would still keep looking at them so as not to give up, because I still needed to move forward. It was through this attentive observation that another form of reading was born in me.

I looked not simply to find, but also and especially to understand. What had really been played out at that border, in that country, by the various protagonists in the scenes captured by the lenses of the Westerners?

A photograph must be considered from its viewpoint. What is given to us to see depends on the material constraints inherent in the production of the image (light, equipment, location . . .)

but also, fundamentally, on the photographer's intention. The subject, the framing and the angle are all subjective choices determined by what he or she wishes to photograph. The reading of an image, its overall understanding, can therefore only be possible by taking account of the identity of the creator of the image. Who is he or she, where are they speaking from and to whom?

What importance does he or she give to the photographs they have taken and what do they do with them in the long term, after their immediate publication by a given media outlet? Does the photographer keep them carefully stored for posterity? To show them to their children, or in the hope of a retrospective exhibition? To give them one day to the people of whose lives they carried a fragment away to the other end of the earth?

At the beginning of my quest, there were the images taken by the B.B.C. journalists. First the "Panorama" documentary, in which a few minutes illustrate some of the moments of our journey and border crossing. I had been able to get hold of that film in early spring 2009. In that sequence, the *préfet* Nsabimana is the only person interviewed. The children and humanitarian aid workers remain silent.

Then, in the spring of 2011, Tony Wende, another B.B.C. journalist, sent me the four photographs he had taken, showing children in the trucks at the border.

In 2020, Alexis Briquet would tell me in our first conversation that there were many other pictures taken that day by the Italian photographer sent by *Terre des Hommes* to document their operation.

I immediately contacted the photographer, Mauro Parmesani, who confirmed over the telephone that he did have some photographs, around 150 of them.

I tried to situate these photographs and videos in the overall image that the West constructed of my country in 1994. What place might they occupy? They were not taken by and for Rwandans. Now that I think about it, I do not believe there was a single photograph taken *by* us or *for* us at the time. They were destined for the rest of the world. The world was watching us through its journalists, its photographers, its humanitarian aid workers. I imagine that those of us who were aware of being photographed back then must have been hoping that those pictures would save us, because their existence was proof that the world knew what was happening in our country, and it could not stand idly by, could it? The world was going to react, wasn't it, to stop the killings? All it would take was the will to do so and a few correctly armed and mandated individuals to put an end to the massacres.

Nothing of the sort happened. The world was content to watch us die on glossy paper and on television. And were it not for the existence of a few foreigners, and of some Hutu people who hid us, resisting the injunction to kill, were it not for the victory of the R.P.F. military, we would have completely disappeared. And after watching us with eyes wide shut, the world would have moved on.

Long after 1994, it was from that perspective that the world continued to see us. Foreigners were the only ones who had captioned the photographs they had taken of us. Their gaze, their interpretation, became our official history.

But today, between the world and us, it seems to me another history is possible at last. And that it is up to us, yesterday's victims, to tell it.

Has not the time now finally come, thirty years after the events, for us to reappropriate those photographs, to caption them ourselves, in our own language, in the light of our own experience?

I felt the need to slip through to the other side of the mirror to change the narrative, to give it more complexity. And instead of the blunt "children fleeing the Rwandan genocide", I wanted to write a story that would say something of the depth of our lives, one that would include our names, our journeys, our hopes and disappointments. One which would say how arduous it is to walk the paths of memory, how difficult to find lost traces of our lives in the archives sleeping in Europe, or those of the International Criminal Tribunal, which are all too often inaccessible.

Bordeaux, late summer 2021

After the death of Alexis, his partner Deanna Cavadini made plans to come to visit me in Bordeaux, in September. She was the one who proposed that Mauro should join us so that he too could meet me and bring the photographs he had in his possession.

The telephone conversations I had previously had with the photographer had led me to imagine a rather voluble man, who seemed to have been profoundly marked by his Rwandan experience.

As a freelance photographer, up until then he had produced reports for travel magazines on luxury hotels or idyllic landscapes at the four corners of the planet. I understood that his partner at the time, Patrizia Miazzo, a newspaper journalist, had convinced him to work for a short period with *Terre des Hommes* Italy, of which Deanna was the delegate general. Before Rwanda, he had completed missions of the same kind in Ethiopia, Benin and Lebanon.

When I first expressed the wish to see the photographs, Mauro had said that from memory there were about 150 of them, in the form of slides in a box, which he had left with his sister and his mother along with all his other archives. He had told me he would gladly give them all to me, as he understood it was an important moment in our lives. I remember he also said, in his French sprinkled with Italian: "I think that what you are doing is very beautiful, for you are working to bring back the memory of that history." He had told me that he had only photographed one convoy, the one on June 18, for soon afterwards he had put aside his camera to give more concrete help to the humanitarian aid workers.

He said he had lost touch with Alexis and Deanna for two decades and that it was after my approach that they had contacted him again. At the time of this telephone conversation, Italy was still in partial lockdown, but he promised me that he would go as soon as possible to collect the box that had been sleeping in the garage at his sister's, in the village near Milan where she lived, and would digitise them and make a selection to send me. That was at the start of 2021.

And yet, when he arrived in Bordeaux, in September that year, in other words more than eight months later, he brought a book of photographs of deserted and silent streets he had taken of the city of Milan during the lockdown, but none of the slides from Rwanda that I was hoping for. I had gone to pick up Deanna at the train station, three hours before the photographer's arrival at the airport. When I told her that, in response to an anxious message of mine, Mauro had admitted a few days earlier that he had not been able to get the box of photographs from 1994, the former humanitarian aid worker expressed her surprise and disappointment, which reflected my own.

I tried to insist on my visceral need to see those images, without offending the photographer, while also putting all my energy into being a good hostess. When he left, he promised once again to do what was required. The photographs were somewhere in the many boxes he had stored with his family over the years, because of his frequent moves.

In the months that followed, he regularly sent me photographs from the reporting he was doing in magnificent locations, but not a single image of the convoy. I champed at the bit, but I kept the lines of communication open.

Why was he taking so long? When he was the one who had recognised that it was "an important time in your lives . . ."

When I prompted him again, he promised he would take care of it after the Christmas break.

Milan and Bordeaux, spring 2022

At last, in March, I got a message from Mauro saying he had selected 76 slides that he was going to digitise. A week later, he sent me a link to download the photographs. I opened the folder, my heart bursting.

There were pictures of dozens of children photographed at the Karubanda school in Butare, in the trucks of the convoy, at the border or in the transit camp in Burundi. On a few rare photographs, I managed to read the names written on the labels pinned to their shirts: did Emmanuel Bigilimana or Alain Ntwali know that photographs of them were sleeping in a box in Italy? The profile portrait of a little boy whose terrible thinness makes it difficult to guess his age particularly captured my attention: the child's cheek is completely slashed. The machete blow he must have received also cut his ear in two. The label shows his name is Éric Shema. Did he survive all that violence? Where might he be today? Although it was an emotional moment for me, my first look at the photographs was nevertheless disappointing: I could not see my face or my mother's on any of them. When I told my husband this, he asked to see the photographs. And it was at that moment, as I was scrolling through the images on my computer screen, that my eye was caught by two silhouettes on a photograph showing a large group of children crossing the border, in the no-man's-land separating the barriers between Rwanda and Burundi.

The photograph is backlit, the children's faces – around 40 of them – are very dark, they are walking on the road towards the photographer, in other words towards Burundi. On the right, on a verge separating that road from the road into Rwanda, there is a large sign saying "*Le Rwanda vous souhaite la bienvenue*" or "Welcome to Rwanda". How ironic! In the crowd of little children, who all have a white label stapled to their clothing on their chest, two White men are clearly visible, one in profile, who is tall, with a light-coloured shirt and trousers, and a bucket hat on his head, the other, shorter, wearing a blue T-shirt and shorts. I had no memory of them. No doubt they were part of the reception committee from Bujumbura.

As I zoomed in, the image lost clarity with each mouse click, but this gave me the impression that I was walking into the depth of the photograph, as I pointed a trembling finger to show my husband the two silhouettes that had startled me: "There! That's Maman and me!"

You have to know what to look for to be able to see it. But I knew. Two very thin people, one with light skin, her hair tied back and a curly fringe, the other with an afro held in by a scarf, and especially the fact that she is wearing the red sweatshirt that my mother had on during the border crossing. Yes, that was us, I was sure of it.

All at once the resentment I had developed towards Mauro vanished. What did it matter that he took so long to digitise the slides, it was worth waiting for! I called him immediately to express my gratitude. I did ask him though, knowing that he had "made a selection" if there were any other photographs in the same series. I suggested travelling to Milan to do the work of digitising them myself to avoid wasting any of his time. He told me that those were all he had.

I did not press him, at the time, and came back to the examination of that photograph. It still had things to reveal to me. On the left, on the edge of the sealed road, almost on the same horizontal line as my mother and me, by zooming in again you can vaguely see a small group of White people. I recognised them. Two of them have light-coloured hair, blond or red, one has headphones on his head and a pole in his hand, the other is leaning over a big black box. Tony the sound recordist and Glenn the cameraman. The third man standing a metre away from them has dark hair and is wearing sunglasses and the same light-blue shirt as Fergal in the B.B.C. "Panorama" report.

The camera is pointed precisely at the border post that Maman and I have just walked past. There was no possible doubt, they must have filmed us. Even if it no longer existed, even if it had stayed in the form of rushes in a forgotten carton, even if it was thrown out after its broadcast in a television news bulletin a few days after June 18, the scene that I had been looking for for almost fifteen years had in fact been filmed.

None of this was a figment of my imagination, nor were the people who claimed to have seen us on television in June 1994.

Mauro had told me there were no more slides in that series. And yet, I had the impression that I had already seen this photograph somewhere . . . It took only a few minutes for the memory to come back to me. It was in an article published by an Italian magazine of which Deanna had sent me the scanned pages a few months previously. At the time I did not know the magazine's publication date or even its name, which did not appear on the pages I received. Was it really the same photograph? The article, signed by Mauro and Patrizia, is called "Rwanda: The Diary of a Rescuer of Children". It contains several photographs, including one slightly larger than a credit card, taken from the same angle as the series that Mauro had just sent me.

When I first received the copy of the article, I had not looked at that photograph closely enough; I had concentrated on the other larger ones and been mostly concerned with having the text translated from Italian. But that evening in March 2022, I re-examined it intensely, comparing it to the one I had received a moment ago. It was not exactly the same image. Mauro must have taken them within a few seconds of each other. In the image from the magazine, there are fewer children, for most of them had probably already reached the barrier into Burundi; the young White man in the blue shorts is almost in the foreground and is carrying a small child in his arms; my mother and I have advanced five paces towards the photographer. It seems I had thrown a jumper over my shoulders, on top of my white T-shirt, and my right hand is raised towards my mouth, as if to stifle a yawn or in a gesture of disbelief. If I could only manage to get hold of the original of this photograph, in a bigger format and higher resolution, I would certainly be able to see our faces and gestures clearly.

I allowed some time to pass and wrote again to Mauro in Milan, insisting this time: are you sure there are no other photographs in this series, such as those that were published in the press? "No, I have sent you everything I have, you would have to ask *Terre des Hommes*, I gave them all of my slides."

I then decided to go back to the B.B.C. In the photograph Mauro sent, I could clearly see the team of journalists filming at the barrier we had just passed. There was no possible doubt that they had filmed us.

But before that, I sent the photographs to the few children of the convoys with whom I was in contact, so that they could see whether or not they appeared in them. Only Claire answered, saying that she recognised her little sister Dadi, in one of the rare individual portraits. The girl, who must be around eleven or twelve, is wearing a purple and black pullover knotted around her shoulders over a brightly coloured top. She has a typewritten label stapled to it on which her name is clearly legible. Dadi also appears in another group photograph, taken just after she had walked past the first barrier at the border.

I had found Claire again quite by chance, the kind of chance only Fate can offer, in the autumn of 2005. I had just moved to Ottawa, following my husband who was doing post-doctoral study at the National Research Council of Canada. I had a meeting in the shopping mall in Rideau Street with a Rwandan woman who had returned from the country with a letter someone had given her for me. Claire had seen us there by coincidence, in one of the vast walkways of the mall. She knew the young woman and greeted her, then, as she held out her hand to me, she exclaimed: "I know this child, but where from?" A few seconds were necessary for our memories to lead us back to June 1994, to the time when she and her sisters had looked after me in the Karubanda school dormitory.

CLAIRE UMUTONI, nicknamed Fifi (convoy of July 3, 1994) and her sisters: ALICE and NOËLLA (convoy of July 3, 1994), MARIE-CHANTAL, nicknamed Dadi (convoy of June 18, 1994), and JOSETTE (probably convoy of June 6, 1994)

In 1994, Claire (nicknamed Fifi by her family and friends since childhood) was seventeen and the eldest of a family of five girls. With their parents, a couple who were upper middle class, the family lived in Rango, one of the residential neighbourhoods in the outskirts of Butare.

When the genocide started, their uncle and aunt in Kigali managed to send their cousins to stay with them. They thought that the killings would not spread as far as the southern prefecture, which had a reputation for moderation. But one day Claire's father received a telephone call from someone unknown telling him, "Your time is up, we're coming to get you," as the Tutsi houses on the hill across from theirs were starting to burn. The parents then decided to send the children to take refuge with an aunt (the widow of their paternal uncle, who was living with a Swiss man, the one named Sunnier).

Fifi recently told me, during an evening in Ottawa we spent remembering those terrible hours, how their mother had accompanied the group of children to the marketplace in Rango before entrusting them to the oldest daughter. Fifi still remembered, thirty years later, what clothes her mother was wearing, and her last desperate look before their separation.

When the Sunnier family was evacuated by Costa and Alexis a few weeks later, they took Claire and the other children to the *Groupe Scolaire*.

Their survival in that place was terribly precarious. Every day militiamen came to kill people, and some of them knew that the daughters of Pierre Rwakayonza were hiding there. They had to duck and dive, spreading the sisters and cousins out in different rooms, and hiding when a kind soul warned them in advance of an attack. Claire also heard later that she and her family were protected by the fact that Alexis had entrusted them in person to the head of the centre. This man, a Hutu, had taken over this "position" after the massacre of the former director (from the Red Cross) and from then onwards it was in his best interests to collaborate with *Terre des Hommes*. In fact, Alexis would later offer him a management role at the centre at the Karubanda school.

During the first evacuation, which left from the *Groupe Scolaire* on June 5 or 6, Claire and her sisters stealthily boarded the trucks. When they got to the border, only the youngest one, Josette, aged twelve, was able to melt into a group that was allowed to cross. Fifi has kept a bitter memory of that night. She saw children older than herself added to the lists by one of the carers from the orphanage, who had his sisters, the wives of Hutu soldiers, pass as escorts who needed to be evacuated. She remembered an officer (I suppose this must have been Colonel Munyengango) in front of the group of people being refused permission to leave, who arranged for their return to take place under guard and who accompanied them to the boarding school, in order to avoid the certain death that awaited them at the *Groupe Scolaire*. The group spent its first night in the boarding school grounds in the cars, because no-one had keys to the buildings.

Fifi told me how, the very next morning, Faustin Rutayisire, a schoolteacher at the Karubanda school (whom she knew quite well, since this was the *lycée* she attended before the genocide), moved into the principal's office and started conducting interrogations of the refugees. He had been named *sous-préfet* of the city by the extremist government. This man's objective was to unmask anyone in the group who was Tutsi, then to hand them over to the militiamen, who would execute them on the other side of the school gates. Claire's name was on the list of those to be executed: Rutayisire was her maths teacher; he had no doubt about her "ethnicity". But the killers were tired that day and the *sous-préfet* went home, telling the condemned that they would be taken care of the next day. That night, Alexis Briquet, who had accompanied the group evacuated to Burundi, came back to Butare. When he found out about the killings perpetrated at the school, he decided to stay until the location was made safe.

*

He also brought them supplies to appease their starving stomachs. Fifi was convinced it was his presence that stopped the killers from coming back.

Josette, the sister who had been able to cross the border, was picked up in Bujumbura by friends of the family who prevented her being sent to a camp in Zaire.

The second sister to leave the country was Marie-Chantal, nicknamed Dadi. She was younger than twelve and was allowed to be part of the convoy on June 18. As I write, she is still the only one who can be recognised in the photographs that I have found.

The three elder sisters and their cousins stayed in Butare until the final evacuation.

After the genocide, the sisters returned to Rwanda. Fifi became the head of the family, even if some of their relatives who had returned from abroad were there too. The third sister, Noëlla, developed serious health issues. She was regrettably not able to receive the care she needed and died four years later.

Alice was the first to go to university abroad. She is now working in Brussels and is married to one of my childhood neighbours and friends. They have two children.

When I found Fifi in Canada in 2005, she was already married and had a son. When she finished her studies, she found a position in the federal government and is currently working in the office of the prime minister of Canada. She lives with her husband and their three children in a francophone city near Ottawa. She brought Josette out to live with her; only Dadi still lives in Rwanda.

Fifi is one of those adolescents who bravely looked after her siblings during and after the genocide, and today she keeps alive the memory of her family and its unity. She fought to find and bury the remains of their parents in Butare and rebuilt the family home so that their past was not completely erased. She is an impressive woman, and I have no doubt that she will soon be able to tell her own exceptional story in the first person.

Bordeaux and London, spring 2022

After the discovery of Mauro's photograph, in which the B.B.C. crew can be seen filming us on the border, I decided to look for images in the B.B.C. archives.

In June 2021, Fergal and his French partner Alice Doyard, a multiple award-winning documentary producer, had come to film me at home in Bordeaux for a documentary on post-traumatic stress syndrome, which affected the famous reporter. I had agreed to speak about our encounter in Rwanda during the genocide, about how I had found Fergal in London, and about my own personal reconstruction after the genocide.

At the time, I had not seen Fergal since 2009, although we had occasionally been in touch, mostly in writing.

The documentary was broadcast in spring 2022 as part of the B.B.C. "Horizon" series. As its title – "Fergal Keane: Living with P.T.S.D." – indicates, it is the Irish journalist's account of how this psychological condition has poisoned his life for more than two decades.

My husband found a way for me to watch the film on the B.B.C. website. It shows Fergal, on the train taking him to Bordeaux, watching the report they had filmed in Butare during the genocide for the first time since 1994. When I saw this, I understood that it was a painful but necessary experience for him.

Following some footage of our meeting at my home, he presents the conversation we had as a source of inspiration for him. He says that what I told him about the necessity of confronting the past while making space for the good things life has to offer will be useful to him in his own healing process.

I knew Fergal was still fragile, so after viewing the film it was to Alice that I wrote to tell her about the new certainty that Mauro's photograph had brought me.

In a message sent six months earlier and to which I had received no reply, I had asked her if she might be able to do some research in the B.B.C. archives, to which I imagined she must have easy access, to check whether the rushes of the "Panorama" film had been kept.

So I followed up in spring 2022, sending her Mauro's photograph and informing her that I would be getting in touch with Rizwana Hamid, the journalist who had organised the reporting in Butare, and who was also interviewed in the P.T.S.D. documentary.

Alice replied to me directly this time, from Ukraine where she was filming:

Fergal and I and the super researcher/assistant producer of the film on P.T.S.D. have fervently searched for the images you mentioned.

We consulted the archives of the B.B.C., watched hours of rushes, but were not able to find them.

This does not mean that they do not exist somewhere. But our search on our side has not been successful.

I am very sorry for not replying earlier and more precisely on this subject. I would have preferred to bring you good news.

Rizwana Hamid, for her part, suggested that I fill in an online form that the B.B.C. has set up for people wishing to obtain a copy of a report in which they appear.

I did so, but with no success.

As for Glenn, the South African cameraman, the message I sent him on Instagram remained unanswered.

I wondered whether I was starting to annoy people with my story.

There was still Tony, who was always approachable. When I told him about all my disappointments, he said he was surprised that his colleagues in Europe had not found anything and concluded, resignedly, that the images I was looking for may have ended up in a rubbish bin, during the period when media organisations threw away many cassettes when they went digital.

Bordeaux and Lausanne, summer–autumn 2022

This was a crucial moment in my quest. I was overwhelmed by contradictory feelings. Sadness at not having been able to conclude my research with the B.B.C., joy at having found Mauro's photograph published in an Italian magazine in 1994, even if it was indistinct and badly framed, but also frustration at the thought that somewhere – but where, damn it? – there were other, clearer ones.

Why could I not just be happy with what I had already found?

Did the fact that I was the only person able to affirm with certainty that those two figures in the photograph were indeed my mother and me prevent me from having a sense of closure? You can barely see our heads over the group. Anyone who did not know the story could say: what is there to prove that's really you in the picture?

And then it took me a while to identify precisely what my expectation was, to understand that the reason I was so determined to find that original image was because I wanted to examine our faces at the exact moment when we crossed over to the side of life. Did they express our fear of the soldiers and militiamen who can be seen in the background, of those who were watching us escape? Did they express relief? Joy? When we spoke over the telephone, Alexis Briquet told me he remembered me clearly from that day. He said something that seemed completely incongruous to me: that I was all smiles. How could

I possibly have been smiling in those terrible moments? All I can remember is an intense feeling of terror. Was it only at the end of our long journey that I relaxed? Was it when we left the country that I started smiling? I could see something that looked like Alexis's profile behind our backs. I knew from the B.B.C. documentary that he stayed at the barrier for a moment, next to *préfet* Nsabimana, watching us walk away. Could that smile he said I wore have therefore been the last expression I offered my country before fleeing it? I wanted to set my mind at rest.

And so I went back to knock on the door of *Terre des Hommes* again. In 2020, my request for access to the list of children in the convoy had not been successful, but maybe they would allow me to look for this photograph?

At the beginning of the summer of 2022, I contacted the person in charge of the archives at the N.G.O.'s offices in Lausanne. I told him about my latest progress, my certainty that a photograph existed. I wrote:

> I know you have already told me that there was no information you could give me about the convoy from the archives of the canton of Vaud. But maybe those photographs have been preserved elsewhere?
> Unless they are located in the *Terre des Hommes offices in Italy?* In which case, would you be able to give me the contact details of the right person to ask to find them?

Something was set in motion, slowly.

The archivist went one more time to the archives of the Vaud canton to try to find "my" photograph. He wrote to me a few days later to tell me that he was able to find the series produced by Parmesani, in the form of a collection of slides. Unfortunately, he regretted to inform me, he did not find the exact item from the newspaper article that I had sent him. He said that there were two slides missing from the collection and that in their place was a card mentioning a loan to various newspapers of the time; he suggested that the photograph was never returned to the N.G.O. He added that he was nevertheless able to identify four other slides taken very close to the time when the group crossed the border, and that he had made a request for copies to be made by the canton archives so that they could digitise them and send them to me by e-mail as soon as possible. He told me in the same message that he was leaving his job that week and that in future I would have to communicate with another person in the organisation.

Once again, a disappointment followed by a new hope. Maybe one of those four pictures that would soon be sent to me would be an image taken a few seconds after the one that had disappeared? Where my mother and I might be in the foreground?

More waiting.

A month later, an archivist from the canton of Vaud sent me a message to let me know that, because of technical difficulties, the organisation no longer had the means to digitise the slides. The photographs would be sent to me only after the problem had been resolved.

The four photographs that were sent to me two weeks later do indeed show scenes from the evacuation on June 18, but none of them are part of the series that I received in March from Parmesani in Milan.

*

I was *not* going to give up so close to my goal.

I made so bold as to ask, now that I was in direct contact with the guardians of the treasure: "Could I possibly come in person to see the slides relating to the *Terre des Hommes* programme in Rwanda in June 1994?"

After another series of e-mail exchanges with the archives of the Vaud canton and my new contact at the *Terre des Hommes* headquarters, the latter finally wrote to me: "We cannot unfortunately grant you access to the archives for reasons of confidentiality."

That refusal might have signalled the end of my investigation, but it brought me just the right dose of anger I needed to pick up my telephone and ring the lady in Lausanne directly. How could they prevent me from having access to a photograph of myself?

The woman listened to me defending my case for a long time. At the end of my monologue, I heard her soft voice with its Swiss drawl tell me she would plead on my behalf with her managers to ask if I might – exceptionally – be given access to the archives.

I do not know what weighed in my favour. Was it my account of a quest spanning several years, my status as a writer with a certain public exposure, or the plans for a book I mentioned? Was it because that woman, who I later learned was responsible for managing the data of the children adopted in Switzerland thanks to *Terre des Hommes*, was more sensitive than my earlier contact? I still have no idea. I can't stop thinking that someone other than me might have had that first refusal upheld, had they not had the arguments of a writer, had they not had the means to get on a plane to Lausanne. I believe the obstacles would have been unsurmountable and discouraged many others.

In early spring 2023, at last, I was able to go to the headquarters of the humanitarian organisation and specifically to the archives of the canton of Vaud.

In the meantime, two essential encounters strengthened my determination to find the traces of our history, to find them in order to be able to share them more widely.

Kigali, spring 2023

DAMAS DUKUNDANE (convoy of July 3, 1994)

    At the beginning of March 2023, I went to Rwanda for a book reading at the invitation of the *Rencontres du Livre Francophone*. I made the most of the trip to meet Damas Dukundane, a doctor from Kigali about whom my friend the historian Hélène Dumas had told me, saying he was one of the children from Kaduha who had been taken in by *Terre des Hommes* towards the end of the genocide, after being saved by the German nun Sister Milgitha. My cousin Rafiki, who had worked with Hélène in collecting first-hand accounts of some of the survivors of Kaduha, gave me the contact details for Damas as soon as I arrived in Kigali. I knew that his group of children arrived in Butare after June 18, 1994, and that we certainly had not had any contact with them in the Karubanda school. And yet I wished to share memories of those weeks with him and to hear how the last evacuation came off.

We met in a tea shop in the centre of Kigali after his day at work. Slim, still very youthful-looking, he had a soft voice, a smile tinged with sadness and the gestures of an attentive practitioner.

    My cousin had already told me that he was, like her, the only survivor of his immediate family. Damas Dukundane was eleven years old in 1994. He found shelter with his mother and little brothers and sisters in the church in Kaduha in April. He had the presence of mind to leave them just before the massacre took place there. Left all alone, he wandered around the church and the health centre in Kaduha for a long time, first terrorised, then resigned. The series of situations that put him a hair's breadth away from death, without it taking him, was something of a miracle. The first time he presented himself at Sister Milgitha's door to ask for asylum, she was not able to take him in for there were soldiers present, and that would have put all the other children she was already looking after in danger too. He spent his nights curled up on the roadsides, his days perched on tree branches from where he could observe the militiamen in action. One day, no doubt exhausted and despairing – I imagine him in rags and terribly thin – he collapsed near a militia roadblock. A scene was then played out of the macabre and absurd kind that I have heard about so often from those months. The militiamen told the one of their group who boasted of being the greatest killer in the area: "Bet you could knock this one off with a flick of your fingers!" A preposterous challenge. The child was so pitiful that the killers had not even bothered to raise their machetes on him, as they were convinced that he would soon die of hunger anyway. But that day, the worst man among them, the one with the most abhorrent record, did something strange: not only did he spare the boy, but, grabbing him by the scruff of his neck like a puppy, he carried him to the German nun's door, so that she could take him in.

And when that nun decided to leave the country, Damas was on the list of 60 children handed over to the protection of *Terre des Hommes*.

That evening in 2023, nearly 29 years after the events, when I talked to Damas about Alexis Briquet and showed him his photograph, Damas said he remembered him but added: "I know he agreed to be a witness on request from the lawyers for the genocidal *préfet*." I told him about the conditions in which all that took place, and explained how Alexis was a good man, despite that epilogue which I understood might be shocking for survivors. Damas smiled, with no ill will.

He told me that when he had a patient in his oncology practice who was a genocidal prisoner, he was especially careful in examining him and treating him, so that he didn't imagine that his doctor was motivated by any kind of desire for revenge.

We looked at the photographs of the genocide in Kaduha that Hélène Dumas had given us (the ones taken by Sister Milgitha). He didn't remember the dates, said that he had then lost all sense of time. After their evacuation from Butare, in early July 1994, he spent several months in a centre managed by *Terre des Hommes* in Burundi. Then one day he returned to Rwanda, and a new life started for him, the life of an orphaned survivor, one of unspeakable loneliness.

His father was not in Kaduha at the time of the genocide. People later gave him all sorts of different versions of his execution. He will never know which one was closest to the truth. He is now married and the father of three young children of his own with whom he spends much of his time.

As I was showing him the photographs that I succeeded in getting from Mauro, he told me that he had undertaken a search similar to mine a while ago. As he told me about it, I felt a unique feeling of gratitude flood through me. I had the sense that I was at last no longer alone in my quest for photographic evidence.

Damas started by showing me an article on his laptop from an American newspaper published on July 21, 1994. When I saw it, I cried out: "I know that one, I also found it online at the start of my research!" He pointed a finger at his name towards the middle of the page: "I was one of the children interviewed by the journalist." The man in question was American: William

M. Pull.[12] In his article, Bill Pull talks about spending time in an industrial warehouse in Bujumbura which had been hastily transformed into a reception centre for around 300 children brought to Burundi by *Terre des Hommes*. He quotes the words of a Hutu teenager who was evacuated with the other handicapped children from the centre in Gatagara, and of a Tutsi girl who survived the genocide in Butare. He says that Damas' story is one of the saddest he heard. He writes that the child hopes to return to Rwanda when that is possible, to study mathematics. The reporter of course puts himself in the picture too: he says that the children, although silent and unsmiling, surrounded him so that he, the visitor, could give them a hug.

I looked at Damas with questions in my eyes. He explained that he remembered that journalist very well, and that the children, who did not speak English, had nicknamed him "Mister Perfect" because he and his wife Brenda Pull[13] asked them to pose for photographs and every time he was happy with the shot, he said "Perfect!"

Many years later, when Damas had become a doctor, he became acquainted with a journalist working for the same American newspaper as Bill Pull in 1994. It was she who told him about the article in which he was quoted. That was how he found out the real name of "Mister Perfect". He did not have much trouble finding him on Facebook and quickly made contact with him. Damas then told me that he and Bill Pull communicated several times via Facebook Messenger. Damas had asked the journalist to send him the photographs the couple had taken of him. But instead of doing so, Pull sent him a link to the Amazon.com page of the book he wrote about Africa. Rather than take the trouble of finding those photographs in his archives, he was inviting their subject to buy and read his book!

Then, when Damas insisted, Pull referred him to Brenda, his wife: "Send her a friend request on Facebook and write to her." The young doctor had even less success with her: she simply never replied, although her account was indeed active.

This story astounded me.

When I got back to France, I went and looked at Bill Pull's C.V. online, to get an idea of who he was. After starting out in journalism, notably in Rwanda and Burundi, he gained a Ph.D. in political science, then became an academic in a university in the American South, working on issues of human rights and activism in Africa. For the last few years, his new research field has been African migrants in Europe, notably those fleeing war-torn countries.

On his Facebook account, he shows himself arm in arm with what he calls "my African friends", human rights activists in Kenya or young sub-Saharan refugees in Italy. I think he still lives with Brenda, who has a flourishing career as a photographer, and he could very well have said to her, one evening over dinner: "We should have a look through some of our boxes of photographs for the ones of the Rwandan children we took in 1994, so we can send the portrait we took to that young man who asked us for it."

But nothing.

"Buy my book on Amazon."

Then I remembered that Tony Wende said the same thing when we talked two years previously. I bought his books about his journalistic adventures to read the few chapters where he spoke about Rwanda. But at least he sent me his four photographs of the convoy, and the link to an article in which he spoke about my message in 2009. He also took the time to talk to me over the telephone about the few memories he had of the convoy, in what was an emotional conversation.

I considered the contents of the book that Bill Pull was trying to sell to Damas, and found out that, quite apart from the caricatural presentation of the history of Rwanda, the author had chosen, as a way of illustrating the genocide of the Tutsi, to tell the story of a non-extremist Hutu he had met in exile in Kenya in November 1994!

Bill and Brenda never deigned to tell Damas whether or not they had any photographs of him in their archives; they did not even look for them. I suppose they are the kind of Westerners who say they love Africa, but only love it if the Africans stay quiet in their assigned roles and let foreigners tell their stories in their stead.

When I left Damas, I thought about those words I had read a few years earlier in the beautiful novel by Abdulrazak Gurnah, *By the Sea*, pronounced by a disabused African exile in Europe imagining someone of Pull's ilk: "An expert in my *area*, someone who has written books about me no doubt, who knows all about me, more than I know about myself. [. . .] He will have slipped in and out of my *area* for decades, studying me and noting me down, explaining me and summarising me, and I would have been unaware of his busy existence."

Damas, for his part, is all too aware of having been the subject of someone else's good story to tell. Mister Perfect simply never foresaw that the little Rwandan orphan would become a brilliant physician, trilingual and well connected, capable of one day claiming what had been taken: a photograph, an element of personal memory.

A few days after this interview with Damas, I visited the Genocide Memorial in Gisozi with Mbougar Sarr, a Senegalese writer who had, like me, been invited to the Kigali book fair. Towards the end of the visit, when I was waiting for him near the exit of the last room, I started a conversation with one of the employees. I had noticed that the panels about the Armenian genocide, which used to be in the room about the other genocides, were no longer there, and I wanted to know why. The man told me they were being updated, and I didn't insist, aware that this might be a delicate subject, given the diplomatic influence of Turkey in the country. After answering more of my questions, the guide finally asked me how I happened to know so much on the subject of genocide. When I told him I was a survivor from Butare, he insisted on introducing me to one of his colleagues who he said had survived in the same city. I hesitated to follow him, afraid of keeping my colleague Mbougar Sarr waiting after he finished his visit.

That would have been a mistake, for then I would not have met that other staff member: Willy Wasungu. As it does every time survivors meet, the conversation quickly turned to how we were rescued. Imagine my surprise to discover that he and his sisters were part of the *Terre des Hommes* convoys!

*

WILLY WASUNGU, DELPHINE UMUHOZA and JOSELINE UMUBYEYI (convoy of June 18, 1994)

In 1994, Willy was nine years old. He had two sisters, one who was ten, the other five, as well as a little baby brother who was still on his mother's breast.

When the genocide started, their father Gakawa, an educated Tutsi of Butare, was quickly killed. Their mother, who was also a Tutsi, went to seek refuge with her sister, whose husband was none other than Joseph Kanyabashi, the head of the town council.

Willy said he did not clearly remember the events that led them to the *Terre des Hommes* centre, but suggested I contact his elder sister Delphine Umuhoza, who, he explained, attached a great deal of importance to memory, as do I. Before we parted, he told me I had the same last name as his other sister, "Umubyeyi", and that was enough to connect us even more beyond our common origins and shared experiences of the convoy.

I waited until I was back in France, a few days later, to call the eldest sister of the family. Delphine had been living in the Loire region since 2003. She was married and had a child. She told me again, but in much more detail, how the husband of their aunt took them to the Karubanda school in Butare, and how their mother miraculously managed to go back to her home hill, with her baby on her back, against the stream of Hutu refugees who were leaving the area in advance of the arrival of the R.P.F.

We did not speak of her uncle, the mayor, who played a part in saving them by putting them in the care of the humanitarian aid workers, but who would be arrested as early as 1995 to appear before the International Criminal Tribunal in Arusha.

Initially sentenced to 35 years in prison for genocide, Kanyabashi had his term reduced on appeal, the judges retaining only his criminal responsibility for direct and public incitement to commit genocide in his town by means of a megaphone in May and June 1994.

When Delphine told me about the convoy and gave me the approximate date, my hands started shaking a little. It could well be the case that this family was in the same convoy as I was. I told her about the photographs that Mauro took on June 18, asked her if she wanted to see them. Of course she did! I sent them to her immediately and twenty minutes later, she sent back one of the photographs showing four rows of children standing in one of the sports fields of the Karubanda school, where the humanitarian aid workers no doubt assembled them before departure, a photograph on which she had added yellow arrows to show me three children. "That's me. I found myself! That's Willy. That's my little sister. Thank you so much."

I had often doubted there was any meaning to my search. I had wondered whether looking for those images might seem futile to some people, whether it would not have been a more rational use of my time and energy to work on other fights for memory and justice. In that night of March 19, 2023, the yellow arrows drawn by that survivor who had just found a personal document of her family, shortly before they left their country, convinced me that what I was doing was not in vain, that it was not just a self-centred flight of fancy by a writer who had been too influenced by the West.

Those images belong to us. It is high time they are returned to their rightful owners.

Lausanne, spring 2023

A few weeks later, I arrived in Lausanne, armed with the courage of a pirate, filled with excitement at the prospect of finding the entire collection of 150 slides that Mauro had mentioned, and, among them, the photograph published by the Italian magazine in which my mother and I are almost in the foreground.

The employee of *Terre des Hommes* who had obtained permission from the canton of Vaud for me to be granted exceptional access to the archives was no longer working there, but she had taken the trouble of putting me in contact with another staff member of the N.G.O., Jean-Luc Imhof, who became a valuable new ally in my quest. When the genocide started in 1994, Jean-Luc had been working for a year for the I.C.R.C. in Rwanda. He was one of those who were evacuated in mid-April. He returned to the country a few months later, this time with *Terre des Hommes*. That was where he met his future wife, a young Tutsi survivor, and her daughter, whom he adopted. His second trip to Rwanda was also a short one because *Terre des Hommes* was forced to leave the country in 1995.

Perhaps because the history of the genocide was now connected to his own family, Jean-Luc immediately recognised the importance of my search and became a generous and sympathetic source of support.

Making the most of my presence in Lausanne, he suggested I come to tell the story of the convoys to his colleagues, as part of one of the sessions of review and appraisal of the field operations that the employees of the headquarters generally organised every week.

This was how I found myself giving my personal account to around twenty humanitarian aid workers, who had almost all joined the organisation after the episode of the genocide (some of them were not even born at the time), with the exception of Ariane Zwahlen and Jean-Luc.

They listened to me attentively, some even said how moved they were by what I shared with them. Some of them had heard of Alexis, but few of them knew him personally. For everyone there, what was happening was a rare event: the presence at the N.G.O. headquarters of what they call a "beneficiary of an operation" several decades after the fact. Someone who had later chosen the same profession as theirs and who also understood its associated constraints and setbacks.

All of them realised that the job had changed so much since 1994, such that what Alexis and Deanna had accomplished could not even be considered today. Their N.G.O. is now required to respect a whole range of security procedures and operational regulations, and to work within a strict framework in which the two humanitarian aid workers – who had not graduated with an aid project management degree and had no other procedural guidelines other than their huge courage, reckless determination and strong hearts – would have no place.

It would take two visits to the Vaud canton archives to get to the end of my search. Two visits for which I would have to send in advance an official and justified request for consultation of the N.G.O.'s documents, and for which, each time, Jean-Luc would need to accompany me to act as guarantor for *Terre des Hommes*.

The world of archives was a new one for me, with procedures I needed to learn: finding the exact call numbers of the documents I was looking for, filling out little forms to give to the archivists, patiently waiting for them to bring me boxes or envelopes on a cart, putting on gloves before touching photographs . . . I thought about the other children of the convoys several times, many of them now living in Rwanda again. Most of whom probably lead precarious lives, surviving with untreated trauma. I know how exceptional the lives of Damas, Claire, Manzi and Annick are, and how they should not allow us to forget about the fragile, broken lives of the majority of the survivors since 1994. How many of my former fellow escapees would have the means to go on this long and tedious quest, full of closed doors and impenetrable rules, in order to find the fragments of their lives that are sleeping here in well-guarded filing cabinets in Switzerland?

I thought of the other children again when I found a white envelope with the word "Kaduha" written on it in blue ballpoint. A few weeks earlier, Damas had told me how his attempt to secure a photograph of himself from a couple of American journalists had failed. So I examined these photographs carefully, scanning the children's faces on the black and white pictures in the envelope. The pictures were no doubt taken on the arrival from Kaduha of the little survivors, who were transferred to the Karubanda school in Butare on June 27. In one of the photographs, around 40 children are sitting in the grass, near a classroom building. Most of them are looking at the photographer, attentive or worried. I hardly dared imagine what their eyes had seen a few weeks earlier: the execution of their families. Fear had nested inside them for a long time to come. And there, on the right-hand side of the third row, his legs crossed and his hands in his lap, wearing canvas trousers and a pullover, I thought I recognised him: Damas. Was it him? A fine scar on his right temple, he is frowning a little, seemingly wondering what the photographer wants of them.

I photographed the whole black and white series, and as soon as I was in the train leaving Lausanne, I sent Damas the photograph in which I thought I recognised him. Like Delphine a few days earlier, I drew a coloured arrow pointing at his face on the picture. I explained that I had just come out of the archives of *Terre des Hommes* and asked him if he was the child indicated by the arrow. A few seconds later, he replied in Kinyarwanda: "That's me." Then in English: "Oh my God, send me more." I sent him the whole series. There were also pictures taken in Burundi, in what was, I assume, the reception centre where the children spent a few months. His laconic "Oh Lord" arrived immediately and conveyed all his emotion. I imagined him in a break between two consultations in Kigali, receiving these traces of his past for which he had been searching for so long. Then he went back into French to thank me heartily for sharing and to tell me how much it meant to him. I asked after his present state: was this not unsettling for him? Maybe I did not take the necessary precautions to prepare him for seeing those images. He replied that he was solid. I know that he later shared these pictures with the other children, that they spent long minutes trying to recognise everyone's faces. The next day I was contacted by Fidèle, the leader of the organisation for the survivors of Kaduha, who sent me a group photograph of the children brought into the world by the now grown-up survivors who arrived in Butare on June 23. A generation later, life has gained the upper hand once more. And the memory of the rescue carried out by Sister Milgitha, then by *Terre des Hommes*, has been passed down, with gratitude.

As I am writing these lines, I still have not found the original of the photograph published by the Italian magazine in which I appear. Mauro, the photographer who took it, told me that after five house moves, his archives were scattered but he would continue to search for the other slides from Rwanda.

Likewise, I have never been able to find out whether the video filmed by the B.B.C. crew, in which my friends say they saw us, still exists somewhere. Maybe in the recesses of the archives of the Residual Mechanism of the International Criminal Tribunal?

I have done as much as I possibly can.

I do, however, have the consolation of having been able to send Damas and Delphine their own images. I also hold fast to the hope that this book will allow me to find other children from the convoy of June 18 and as the years go by to give them the few mementos that I have been able to collect over my fifteen-year-long quest.

I like to think that my work might, modestly, be able to contribute to the enormous task faced by the Rwandan survivors who wish to produce knowledge about themselves and have worked towards making the archives of the genocide accessible. In 2022 Hélène Dumas introduced me to the team of archivists that she had assembled to do this with Ibuka Rwanda. During gatherings in offices adjoining the Nyanza-Kicukiro Memorial in Kigali, this group of survivors worked for more than a year to produce an archive from the thousands of documents the organisation had collected since 1995. I was able to see them toiling away in that huge room in their white coats, sorting and filing those precious documents collected from all the hills of the country by the members of Ibuka, notably by the paralegals and the mental health workers who had had the courage, when they were bereaved themselves, to go and collect those eyewitness accounts.

Those archives, which benefited from the support of the Shoah Memorial in Paris and from the expertise of Hélène Dumas (thanks in part to a grant from the French National Research Agency), have a double vocation. On the one hand, they constitute an indispensable resource for Rwandan and foreign researchers; on the other hand, they are available to survivors wishing to have access to their own history and to be able to pass it down to their descendants.

During my last stay in Rwanda, in the spring of 2023, I visited the new building of the Ministry for National Unity and Civic Engagement, in which several floors were destined to hold the archives relating to the genocide against the Tutsi.

A first training programme for its staff was organised in 2022, as part of a three-year partnership with the Shoah Memorial. In the library that was in the process of being organised, I found several copies of Fergal Keane's *Season of Blood*.

As I left the building, and despite how much remained to be done, I wondered, in hope, whether one day the various traces of the convoys could be assembled here, within reach of all the children who might wish to find them: copies of photographs, lists of names, my account, Annick's and those of others which, I hope, will not fail to arrive.

Beyond the convoys, my investigation led me to ask questions about the fate of the pictures taken by foreign photographers in Rwanda during and just after the genocide against the Tutsi. The many obstacles I encountered were all unexpected opportunities to consider the part that images play in the way we tell, rewrite, remember or forget stories like ours, in a world of inequalities between voiceless protagonists – because they are African? – and the photographers who bear all the influence of the West. I understood that it was the anomalies in the journey that should have been mine that have allowed me to advance as far as I have in my quest: my age when I left, my new life in France, my studies, my knowledge of the world of aid work, my status as a writer, the access I had to all the books that informed my analytical understanding of history, the psychological support and friendship of so many people in France. I was able to benefit from all kinds of means – material, immaterial, human – to which few children from the convoy of June 18 would have been able to get access had they wanted, as I did, to find their photographs.

Thousands of photographs were taken in Rwanda in 1994 by foreigners, mostly journalists and humanitarian aid workers, and sometimes members of religious orders. How many of those are now available, accessible in Rwanda or on the internet, for the survivors who may wish to find them?

They are sleeping in the archives of Western media organisations, of the International Criminal Tribunal, or in the storage boxes of photographers who took them without ever imagining that one day the people who appear on their images could come knocking on the door saying, "You have something that belongs to me and I have come to collect it."

Do those photographs not belong to us?

The photographers, if they are kind like Mauro or Tony, will take the time to help the person search through their boxes. If they are of the ilk of "Mister Perfect", they will slam the door in the face of the stranger. Is this because they are convinced that the person cannot rise above their status as subject, as an extra in a story that no longer belongs to them? Or is it simply indifference, or a contempt arising from not seeing the other as someone capable of appreciating the value of a photograph?

Obviously I believe in the intellectual property rights of photographers. But I cannot help wondering about the rights to those images of the people being photographed. To what extent can we have access to information about the identity of those who *took* our photographs? Or have access to copies of those pictures? And if I take the argument further, to what extent can we have our say about the images of us that are published or broadcast, about the way they are captioned and interpreted to the rest of the world?

In the immediacy and urgency of war, when massacres are taking place, none of those questions are asked, of course.

But afterwards?

During the commemoration of the twenty-fifth anniversary of the genocide against the Tutsi, I was able to observe how this question of the images and the captions in which the protagonists were excluded had not been settled, far from it.

*

I have occasionally asked for changes to be made: of an image (skulls, a mass grave . . .) arbitrarily chosen by a magazine to illustrate the publication of a text I have written, or of a turn of phrase used to review one of my books. I have not always been successful. How many survivors are able to do this?

It was through reading Susan Sontag's *Regarding the Pain of Others* that I was able to put words to the unease I felt in seeing the treatment by some journalists of the most recent commemorations of the genocide. In her essay, Sontag reminds us that the spectators from wealthy nations do not consider the dead and torture victims of Africa in the same terms as those in their own countries, justly underlining that while the Western media did not publish images of the victims of the attacks of 9/11, "postcolonial Africa exists in the consciousness of the general public in the rich world [. . .] mainly as a succession of unforgettable photographs of large-eyed victims, starting with figures in the famine lands of Biafra in the late 1960s to the survivors of the genocide of nearly a million Rwandan Tutsis in 1994".

All those images of us, of our dead, of their remains, continue to be broadcast without our being asked for our opinion.

When Sontag writes later in the same essay, quite rightly, "for the other, even when not an enemy, is regarded only as someone to be seen, not someone (like us) who also sees", she is putting her finger on the question of our own gaze.

And what do I see – I the other, once a photographed victim – when I consider most of the images taken by Western photographers from April to August 1994 to illustrate our history? Why do I feel such profound unease?

I am not speaking here of the photographs of the convoy, but of the others, those I discovered when I first arrived in France and since then.

While the genocide against the Tutsi in Rwanda did not take

place live on television – contrary to what has been claimed all too often – numerous images were produced in the very first days and rapidly published in the world's media. This was a very different situation from that of World War II and even of the genocide perpetrated by the Khmer Rouge in Cambodia nineteen years earlier, when Pol Pot had closed all doors to journalists in order to stop them from documenting what was happening in the country under his control.

To explain the nature of my unease, I had to consider the conditions of production of those photographs or videos. The Ph.D. thesis by a contemporary art historian, Nathan Réra, who analysed twenty years of images produced by journalists and artists on the genocide against the Tutsi, was very useful to me in that regard. Réra also interviewed several photographers and cameramen about their work and how it was broadcast, and also asked more widely about their lives after this singular event that had marked them profoundly. His particularly well-documented study allowed me to articulate the question of the origin of the gaze of Western journalists – who for a long time were the only ones to tell our story – and its relationship with the global narrative of the genocide. I then wondered what it means to speak from a land that, for decades, has been talked about *by* others *to* others. Which only entered the world's awareness through a narrative produced by images taken by outside spectators. Is it possible to imagine that the history of the major Western conflicts, of the Holocaust, of the massacres committed in Europe, might have been told and explained to the world on the basis only of writings, films and photographs created by journalists from Africa or South America who had either "covered" the events, or gathered and rewritten their own versions of the accounts of the Europeans and North Americans?

It is not that men and women from Rwanda have written nothing, far from it, but if you look at the factual accounts that have received the most attention in the world (apart from works of fiction), they are overwhelmingly the work of foreigners who were sent to Rwanda and gathered stories there.

Many of them did so honestly with the intention of providing information, even of denouncing the lack of action or collusion of the Western powers. Most of their work is the result of a serious and respectful approach.

But I hear from more and more survivors who are unhappy with the way their personal, sometimes intimate histories, which they had confided to Western journalists as eyewitness accounts that they were supposed to co-sign, have been written and altered. And I wonder.

In my first novel, *All Your Children, Scattered*, I have one of my characters, who will not allow her husband, a foreigner, to write the story of her mother, a survivor, say: "People who write about us, those who seek to transcribe our silences, without knowing the score: they sometimes lack good manners."

Almost all the French journalists who interviewed me when the book came out asked me to justify this sentence: did I mean that the genocide of the Tutsi should only be written about by Rwandan survivors? After explaining that those were the words of a fictional character, I would answer that I believed anyone could write about that story on the condition that in doing so they were clear about where they were writing from, with which perspective, and without speaking on behalf of anyone else.

But I would also often add that it was important that the accounts of the victims should be at the centre of the collective memory being created in the world since 1994, and that the victims be listened to, and heard.

*

When I first threw myself into the search for images of the convoy, I did not imagine that I would go over to the other side of the lens, to observe the photographers in action. I probably would never have done so if all the doors of the archives had been opened for me, if the authors or depositors of those images had readily given them to me, if I had not become aware that other survivors had been met with categorical refusals. Retrospectively, and even though I am still looking for that one *missing picture* today, I can see my disappointments and failures as beneficial. Without them, I would not have realised the extent of the problem.

When the genocide started in the beginning of April, the first images produced were by reporters who had come to cover the evacuation of expatriates from the capital. This was the Western media's common approach to information about crises in Africa at the time: they showed greater concern for the safety of their own nationals while the fate of the local population was generally summarised in a haze of violence with no analysis of the causes nor details of the profiles of the victims. Only a dozen or so special reporters were sent to Rwanda at the time, since most of the others were busy with events receiving more exposure in the media: the war in Bosnia or the elections in South Africa.

Foreign journalists therefore embedded themselves almost exclusively in the evacuation convoys organised by the Belgian and French para-commandos in order to move around the country. For reasons of security, the journalists therefore saw the situation in Rwanda only through the movements of the European troops they were following. This nevertheless still allowed them to collect a few images that might have been informative about the genocide that was in progress, had they been accompanied by any commentary or adequate captions, or if they had not been used to further a problematic narrative.

Let us remember that in the spring of 1994, the dominant discourse presented the violence as the result of an atavistic hatred between Hutu and Tutsi, which had given rise to repeated conflicts. Neither the reporters on the ground nor the commentators in the television studios seemed to have a sufficient knowledge of the history of this little country, and most of them had scarcely heard of it, if at all, beforehand. This ignorance would allow the political communicators, notably in the French president's office, to spread the notion that two antagonistic camps were battling for power (the national army, exclusively made up of Hutu, against the Tutsi rebels of the R.P.F.) and were collectively responsible for killings "on both sides".

However, one year previously, in January 1993, in front of the millions of viewers of the evening news on the France 2 television channel, the activist Jean Carbonare, who had returned from a mission for the International Federation for Human Rights (I.F.H.R.), had informed public opinion in France about the crimes committed in Rwanda by those in power. He had clearly stated that the victims were from the Tutsi minority, leaving no possible doubt as to the nature of the massacres organised by the authorities.

In 1994 and in the decades that followed, the fact that the group identity of the victims of the genocide was hardly ever mentioned, and that the events were systematically summarised by the consecrated term "Rwandan genocide", allowed the incorrect notion to be spread of a generalised madness where everyone was killing everyone, in a racist vision of a historically violent population.

While there were in fact massacres of non-extremist Hutu in the first weeks, notably of members of the political parties that for years had been opposed to the racist policies of the Hutu Power movement, as was the case with the prime minister on April 7, these were committed by Hutu extremists not Tutsi, and it rapidly became clear, at least to Rwandans, that the official policy was to exterminate all Tutsi, from babies to elderly people.

And yet the first images collected by the reporters following the evacuations, and the way in which they were or were not distributed in Europe, only contributed to a narrative that had no basis in fact.

In his thesis, Nathan Réra cites several remarkable examples of this. I will mention two of them here.

The first is about a series of videos made during the evacuation of European members of religious orders and carers from the only psychiatric hospital in Rwanda, at Ndera, near Kigali.

Hundreds of Tutsi who had taken refuge in the hospital had greeted the Belgian paratroopers with hope, begging them to protect them from the Hutu militiamen who were already crowding at the gates. But in Ndera as in other parts of the country, the soldiers would soon leave with only their European compatriots, abandoning the Tutsi to certain death. When the reporters recorded the words of refugees calling for help in perfectly comprehensible French and showing the corpses of the first victims, this footage was deleted from the reports that were put together and broadcast in France. What was shown was terrorised Belgian members of religious orders, paratroopers shooting into the air – which erroneously made the operation appear dangerous for them – while the future victims were reduced to the role of extras, deprived of a voice.

*

By mid-April, the end of the evacuation of expatriates led to the departure of several reporters. Two photographers, Luc Delahaye and Patrick Robert, chose to stay in the country. They went to document an open mass grave of more than 100 bodies on the hill of Nyanza-Kicukiro, in the outskirts of Kigali, which had recently been liberated by the R.P.F. military. The photographs taken by Patrick Robert could have been the best evidence of the scope of the events since the beginning of the massacres, but the French news magazines refused to publish them, which was not the case in Germany or in America.

As for the film shot by Delahaye, it is a sequence of images less than two minutes long (taken from an hour of rushes) that was broadcast a few days later on the France 3 television channel. The journalist had made sure to include long interviews with a few survivors of the massacre at Nyanza, but there again, as with the psychiatric hospital in Ndera, the victims' accounts were silenced or minimised, in a process which made the crimes taking place difficult for the viewers to understand correctly. Who had killed whom?

Nathan Réra stresses the fact that a single image could be published with two contradictory captions: either the victims were presented as Rwandan refugees with no distinction as to whether they were Hutu or Tutsi, or, when the caption indicated that the victims were killed because of their Tutsi identity, a comment or another image might be included that suggested a possible participation of Tutsi in killings of Hutu.

Confusion would be the line taken by the communication agencies of the French government, who were embroiled in their links with the dictatorial regime that had planned and executed the last genocide of the twentieth century.

*

The Hutu refugee camps were the second theatre of an incredible media misconstruction, which has sometimes endured to this day.

Starting in late June 1994, the French military of *Opération Turquoise* put in place what was called a "humanitarian safety zone" in the south-west of Rwanda, which was to serve as a fallback space for the genocidal authorities, military and militias. It was from that zone that these people were able to organise their flight to Zaire, taking with them more than two million Hutu civilians, including many killers. While the episode of the genocide that had just come to an end may have been covered by only ten journalists, and only a handful of humanitarian aid workers had stayed or come to the rescue of the Tutsi, the Hutu refugee camps attracted hundreds of members of the world's media and one of the largest deployments of humanitarian aid of the century.

Newspapers, radio and television all over the entire planet were flooded with images and accounts of the hunger, thirst, overcrowding and exhaustion suffered by the refugees. The arrival of a cholera epidemic offered the journalists apocalyptic scenes which the international media had no compunction in ascribing to the genocide.

I remember those images. I had arrived in France on July 5, and from the sofa in my host family's living room, I saw this worldwide effusion of sympathy towards those people, who were undoubtedly suffering in that terrible exodus, but also the world's concurrent obliviousness to the crimes that some of them had just committed, thereby insidiously leaving the true victims of the genocide out of the frame.

It was surreal and greatly unsettled me.

Nathan Réra quite rightly stresses that "the dominant iconography of the genocide was consequently composed on the basis of a major misrepresentation, encouraged by the presence of French army bulldozers bearing the corpses of cholera victims to the mass graves dug to receive them". And indeed, there were many people who likened those images of mass graves dug by bulldozers in the volcanic soils of Goma for the Hutu victims of cholera to those filled with the victims of the Bergen-Belsen concentration camp in April 1945. The intense media exposure given to the burial of the bodies of the assassins and their families, killed not by other men but by an epidemic, also buried the reality of the genocide against the Tutsi.

The photographs taken in the refugee camps in Zaire, mostly in the eastern province of Kivu, and Tanzania, notably in the Benaco camp in the north-west of the country, by some of the greatest figures of photo-reportage (James Nachtwey, Sebastião Salgado and Gilles Peress) became, through a terrible misrepresentation, the symbols of the genocide.

And while some journalists have since become aware of their mistake, such as the French television reporter Gauthier Rybinski, many others have continued to publish books or mount exhibitions of photographs that make the cholera epidemic the epicentre of their work on what many people have called the "Rwandan tragedy". Nathan Réra cites *Inferno*, by Nachtwey, *Exodus* by Salgado, and *On a deux yeux de trop* by Anthony Suau (with texts by Florence Aubenas) published after the events. Réra says of the latter two: "These albums have inherited the dialectic of the media, the images tending to renew the most irrepressible stereotypes."

He also talks about how the retrospective exhibition "The Shadow of War" held at the European photography museum, the *Maison européenne de la photographie* in Paris in 2011 only kept two photographs to represent "the genocide in Rwanda": one image of Hutu refugees in a camp taken by Salgado in 1995, and the famous photograph by Nachtwey of the profile of a young Rwandan man whose face is lacerated with machete blows. However, this man was a non-extremist Hutu who had been attacked by Hutu militiamen for refusing to participate in the genocide. This information was correctly given by another photographer who was present in Nyanza, Jean-Marc Bouju, who had also photographed the young man, but whose photograph did not, as Nachtwey's did, win the prestigious World Press Photo of the Year award, nor was it published in a double page spread in *Time Magazine*. In 2013, when this same photograph appeared in the French daily newspaper *Libération*, it was accompanied by a caption which, while not completely incorrect, is at the very least problematic. The injured young man is presented solely as "Hutu with a mutilated face, Rwanda" without explaining by whom and why he was attacked with a machete. On James Nachtwey's official website, he is simply described as a "survivor of Hutu death camps".

Some photographers, however, have become aware of how they completely misrepresented the account of the genocide against the Tutsi, and later tried to initiate projects and make proposals for exhibitions that would tell another story, while at the same time questioning the role of photojournalism.

Christophe Calais was one of these, a French photojournalist who had covered the humanitarian crisis in Zaire for the French magazine *VSD*. He had contributed to the transformation of a little Hutu boy into an "icon of the genocide". The seven-year-old, presumed dead from cholera, had been saved from being buried alive under the bulldozers by a lieutenant of *Opération Turquoise*. The French soldier had looked after him and fed him, going so far as to rebaptise him Angelo.

Réra explains how the photograph had made Calais famous:

"Collective memory will retain the image of Angelo rather than of the little mutilated Tutsi children two months earlier, for it represents the incarnation of a double ideal: a White man, both strong and sensitive, who takes an innocent victim under his wing, and a 'little African boy' who is hungry for life and has seen death (or hell) close up and managed to escape it *in extremis*." It would later be known that the father of the child had participated in the genocide, and that he was denounced by his neighbours when he returned to Rwanda and in due course sentenced to 25 years in prison.

Christophe Calais would later distance himself from the media machine and start a project of many decades documenting another history of the country, in post-genocide Rwanda.

As for Luc Delahaye, he would give this explanation (quoted in *Le Monde*, November 24, 2005) about the only other photograph that he took, ten years after the genocide, on the occasion of the inhumation of 80 victims of genocide in Musenyi: "Taking that photograph was to return to a failure. I greatly regret not having been able to represent the genocide at the time, when I was there for the three and a half months that it lasted. A sense of the powerlessness of images, of their flagrant uselessness. I made that image as if to make amends, or fill a void, or to banish that powerlessness."

In his thesis, Réra endeavours to analyse the differing impact of photographs or videos devised to overcome this "crisis of the image" provoked by the media coverage of the various Rwandan events: those by Alfredo Jaar, Gilles Peress, Alexis Cordess, Sarah Vanagt and others, without failing occasionally to stress the limits of some of those approaches.

*

Those few course corrections have unfortunately not yet managed to put an end to the misuse of the images of Rwandans taken in 1994, and it is to be feared that the occasion of the commemoration of the 30 years since the genocide against the Tutsi may see some of those reflexes persist.

For even when truth has been re-established, the images can remain trapped in the first narrative that was made about them.

I learned very recently that the woman who appears in the famous photograph by Dorothea Lange, "Migrant Mother", which became all by itself the symbol of the exodus of farm workers during the Great Depression, was not who she was said to be. The photographer, sent by a U.S. government programme to document the situation of poor farmers and to promote President Roosevelt's New Deal, had taken this photograph of a woman with her children sitting under a tarpaulin on the side of a Californian road, not far from a camp of migrant workers who were harvesting peas. The photograph would be published by many national newspapers with an inaccurate caption, presenting the woman with the tired expression as one of the workers from the camp who had been forced to sell the tyres of the family car to buy food.

The image touched all of America and it is said that it had the effect of giving rise to considerable food aid being sent to the workers' camp.

It would take years for the children of Florence Owens Thompson – that's the woman's name – to make their mother's real history known. She was not part of the migrant population whose icon she had become. The woman, who was considered a White American, was in fact a descendant of a Cherokee family who had been living in California for more than ten years. It was only chance that had brought her to the field of peas: after their car broke down, she was waiting for her husband and older boys who had gone to the nearby town to make the necessary repairs, before they drove away. Which meant that Florence Owens Thompson and her family did not benefit at all from the food aid that was sent a few days later in response to the publication of her photograph.

The controversy surrounding that incorrect caption, which some people have accused of furthering a "colonialist" gaze, has not prevented the photograph from remaining, in the worldwide collective imagination, the symbol that it was made out to be at the beginning.

After reading Nathan Réra's foundational work, I came back to the images of the convoy of June 18, 1994, that I had in my possession, to reconsider the narratives that had accompanied them – their captions, so to speak.

I listened again to the English commentary by Fergal Keane on the B.B.C. film, and reread the text co-signed by Mauro Parmesani and Patrizia Miazzo in the magazine published in Italy.

The B.B.C. documentary presents the children of the convoy as "Tutsi orphans who would be killed if they stayed in Butare". Which would in fact have been the case for most of them. Before arriving in the zone that was still in the hands of the genocidal government, the Irish reporter had been able to get an idea of the scope of the extermination by interviewing Tutsi survivors in the zone liberated by the R.P.F. He allows them to speak at length in a previous sequence of the documentary.

There was therefore no silencing of the victims, and the journalistic work was rigorous.

Having arrived subsequently in one of the last bastions of Hutu power, Keane did not take the risk of giving the microphone to the victims, and that is understandable. That is why only the *préfet* Nsabimana is interviewed in the later sequence. The voice-over presents him as a brave man who risked his position to save the lives of Tutsi children. Nsabimana for his part – nothing surprising there – doesn't clearly explain what is happening: he talks about the war, about conflicts between adults for which the children "whatever their identity" should not be held responsible. And when Keane asks him what is motivating the killings, he says they are caused by hot-headed individuals, by instances of personal hatred.

As for the Italian article entitled "Rwanda: The Diary of a Rescuer of Children", it talks of a humanitarian rescue "in the country of a thousand hills devastated by the war between Tutsi and Hutu" without saying anything about the real identity of the children, much less that of the killers, and without analysing the political character of the violence, probably because the authors were unaware of either. The same text could have come from any African country in the throes of a civil war. Mauro and Patrizia obviously did not try to provide any political analysis or to situate what they had seen in the context of the history of Rwanda.

The feelings of the rescuer, however, are described at length: his fear of "shootings carried out by strangers and reckless warriors of the night", his emotion at the sad eyes of the children resigned to their fate, his regret at leaving them once the rescue is accomplished, and finally the sense of being radically changed by this experience in which he felt he had been useful.

I have tried to consider this text positively despite its rather caricatural tone, for I believe that Mauro and Patrizia did their best to make themselves useful alongside the humanitarian aid workers, and because I will always be grateful to the photographer for sending me images of the convoy.

Bordeaux, summer 2023

One last lead.

Last week, as I was asking more questions of him, the Milanese photographer gave me the name of the Italian magazine in which his photographs and his article about our convoy had been published, 29 years ago: *No Limits*.

When he told me that the magazine no longer existed, I hastily deduced that there would be nothing more to find in that direction either.

And yet.

All it took was a few clicks to find out what that magazine had been. *No Limits* was part of a sportswear brand of the same name, founded by the "Cavaliere del Lavoro Filippo Giardello, an entrepreneur in the world of watchmaking for 4 of four generations".

The history of the company that I found online shows that the founder then had the brilliant idea "to link the brand to the newborn world of extreme sports, riding the wave of what the marketers of the nineties called 'standardisation of the concept of adventure' [. . .] directly evoking a strong belief in creating a company that seeks its own limits".

Between 1991 and 2001 the magazine *No Limits* thus published hundreds of reportage articles on the practice of extreme sports, but also featured accounts by people who devoted their lives to "a constant search for overcoming his [sic] own limits".

When the magazine ceased publication, the brand created a

"No Limits Library" which, according to the website, "consists, to date, of 1,866 [. . .] films on various media [. . .] equal to 8,000 hours of footage and about 15,000 photographs".

Is this where I would finally find "my" slide? Between the photographs of a solo Atlantic crossing and those of a descent of a volcano on a snowboard?

This improbable epilogue confirms my sense that we should have spoken up long ago to tell our own stories, to caption our own photographs, and to do so in spaces that we deem appropriate, safe and accessible.

A space for us, a memorial for the children of the convoys.

This book lays only the first stone.

Epilogue

We are a multitude, scattered all over the world.

This book has opened so many doors, gathered together so many people. As I was writing it, I hoped that it would allow me to get in touch with other children from the convoys and to find other images. But I never could have imagined how quickly that would happen, beyond even my most optimistic expectations. This book reminded me that literature, when it cuts to the bone and gives body to history, really can transform our lives.

There would be enough material to write a sequel to this first memoir, but, as I clearly stated at the end of *The Convoy*, I hope that people will read the other stories – those by my companions in flight that will surely soon be available – for each singular destiny deserves to be heard.

Eight months after the publication of the book in France, I can draw up a first assessment of its immediate impact. My investigation has continued; it has even accelerated in the most extraordinary way. I have made more progress in 2024 than in fifteen years of research.

The week after the book came out in France, I received a message on a social media platform, sent by Rodolphe. He said that he had been given a copy and that the photograph on the cover had immediately revived an old memory. In 1994, as a young French humanitarian aid worker aged 22, he happened to be in Bujumbura for the N.G.O. Action against Hunger when he and his colleagues received a request from Alexis Briquet to collect children arriving at the border in a convoy from Rwanda.

EPILOGUE

Rodolphe wrote that he had taken several photographs that day and that he was willing to send them to me. As fate would have it, he now divides his life between Washington and . . . Bordeaux. I met him a few days later and he gave me twenty black and white pictures taken at the border. He did not remember the exact date, but on seeing that none of the children had name labels pinned to their clothing, I deduced that this was not the convoy of June 18. Knowing also that the children in the first convoy were all collected by the I.C.R.C., I concluded that these photographs were taken on July 3. I will be sure of this only when I can find someone from those pictures who can identify themselves and confirm that they were part of the last journey organised by *Terre des Hommes*.

I soon heard more about the I.C.R.C. when I received an e-mail from Daniel Philippin, who in 1994 was a delegate of the Swiss agency, also based in Bujumbura, whom I mention on page 169. I later met Daniel in Geneva and we exchanged our books. His was an autobiography of a lifetime of humanitarian aid work, self-published in 2003, which I had been unaware of until then. It includes a chapter on Rwanda. Aged 32 at the time, Daniel had organised significant support from Burundi for his colleagues remaining in Rwanda, including several rescue convoys. He gives a two-page account of his participation in the first convoy from Butare co-ordinated by *Terre des Hommes*. Thanks to him, I now know with certainty that it took place on June 6, for it was on his birthday. While his account differs slightly from that of the Italian consul, Pierantonio Costa, I discovered that it was by dint of a last-ditch negotiation that they managed to extract the children from the clutches of the militiamen massed at the border: their safe passage was secured in exchange for a small truck of medical equipment, mostly bandages.

And then, very soon, the children of the convoys started contacting me.

The first among them, Milan, introduced himself to me at the launch of my book in early January 2024 at a bookshop in Paris. He showed me one of the photographs of the convoy of June 18 that I had posted on the internet and, pointing at a little boy wearing a denim jacket, said: "That's me." Milan explained that he was only four years old at the time, and that it was on account of that jacket of which he retained a vivid memory that he had recognised himself in the picture. I was overwhelmed with emotion at this first reunion. He admitted that he had been following my news on social media for some time, but had not had the courage to contact me until then.

After him, others would do the same, having heard me on the radio or seen me on television.

Bernard, who now lives in Belgium and was eighteen in 1994 when he was a part of the July 3 convoy, found my contact details at the end of January by way of a mutual friend and survivor living in Brussels. Over a long telephone conversation, he told me his memories, which had remained very vivid.

At the beginning of April, I received a message that began: "Umubyeyi, Thank you, from the bottom of my heart. I love you already. I was eight years old in the convoy with my brother who was nine." This was from Clément, who had managed to get my contact details from a childhood friend, an orphan of the genocide with whom he had grown up in Kigali and who was none other than Luck, the son of Karoli, the cook who fed us when we were hiding in the hotel. Luck now lives in Arizona and has become a father himself. He looks so much like Karoli, that father whose features he has forgotten for no photograph of him exists, and he understands more than anyone about our quest for images. Clément confided to me over the telephone that he had often thought about writing his story, that he had even considered making a documentary film with Luck, but that he was missing too much information. "It's as if I could guess that you would come along one day to fill all the holes in our memories at last, that you would give us our reconstituted history." When I sent him the photographs of the convoy of June 18 taken by Mauro Parmesani, he immediately recognised himself with his brother Éric by his side.

That was also the case for the sisters Anne-Marie and Marie-Michelle, respectively aged seven and four during the genocide. They contacted me with the help of their uncle, who had spoken about it to Hélène Dumas, and were also able to find themselves in the photographs from June 18.

And then there was Gloria, who approached me at a Rwandan evening at the *Théâtre Chaillot* in Paris, when she was in France for a short stay. It was Clément, whom she had found again during the commemoration of the genocide in Butare, who had spoken to her about my book. During the genocide, she was four and her brother nine months old. Her memories of the evacuation were hazy, but the presence of buses from the national Onatracom company and of French soldiers did not leave me in any doubt: she was part of the July convoy. No photographs of her have been found, for now.

Not a week goes by without another person approaching me, a child of the convoys or an uncle, or a family friend. In the case of Nadine, who with her sisters was part of the last convoy, it was a Belgian documentary film producer who met her at Liège during a commemoration of the genocide against the Tutsi who put us in contact.

We are a multitude, scattered all over the world.

In March, during a book event in Quebec to which I was invited by *Mémoire d'encrier*, the publisher of my collection of poetry *Culbuter le malheur*, a Rwandan couple introduced me to a tall and reticent man, their cousin Maxime. They had fostered him in 1994, after his rescue by Alexis and Deanna. Maxime was a baby at the time. Someone had saved him after picking him up from beside his mother's dead body. He had received blows to the head that had resulted, unsurprisingly, in his reserved relationship to the world, in his broken life. It was my friend Claire, nicknamed Fifi, who is also now living in Quebec, who had looked after him in Butare before his evacuation by the convoy of June 18. Maxime retains no memory of the convoys, nor of his deceased parents.

In Montreal, at the end of a memorable evening organised by the Page Rwanda organisation, a gentleman gave me the contact details of a friend from Burundi who he said had actively participated in the evacuation of children for *Terre des Hommes*. Adrien now lives in Nicaragua with his family. Over the telephone, he told me of the deep impression that the luminous figure of Alexis had made on him. They had met in 1994 in a Greek restaurant in which the young man was working. Alexis was desperately seeking vehicles to collect the Rwandan children at the border. Adrien explained that many Burundians and exiled Rwandans had been mobilised to help the *Terre des Hommes* delegate, alongside Western humanitarian aid workers. Adrien also later became a volunteer in the reception centre set up in a hangar in the industrial zone of Bujumbura to welcome the children. Very critical of the Western N.G.O.s, he nevertheless retains an admiring memory of Alexis, whom he called "a good man".

Shortly after my return from Canada, I received an unimaginable call from Pierre, who announced that he had perhaps found the B.B.C. film for which I had been looking for fifteen years. I met Pierre and Yvonne, his Rwandan wife and a survivor, thanks to our mutual friends the historians Jean-Pierre Chrétien and Hélène Dumas. As a young French volunteer posted to Butare, Pierre had lived through the genocide in 1994 with Yvonne by his side. After reading my book, Pierre had decided to find the B.B.C. rushes with the help of a former colleague in the International Tribunal for the former Yugoslavia in The Hague, where he and his wife had worked. That was how, at the beginning of April, he came to send me two videos of a few minutes each. The V.H.S. films made by the B.B.C. journalists in 1994 had been digitised and the hard disks on which they were recorded had been sleeping on a shelf in the archives for two decades. The images were of poor quality, the sound patchy, but in one of them, in the background of an interview with the *préfet* Nsabimana, I recognised myself in the middle of a group of children waiting at the border. Further on in the recording, I was also able to locate my mother and me in the little crowd of escapees in the convoy heading for Burundi. I was overwhelmed to receive these images. They were too short for me to be able to distinguish the emotions on our faces, but they revived a few very precise memories. I saw myself picking up a small child and carrying him or her for the last few metres separating us from deliverance. Maybe one day I will find that child who holds the other half of that memory, which we will be able to fit together like two pieces of a puzzle.

I effusively thanked Pierre, Yvonne and their friend. On the video, I was also struck to see that another person, to whom I had until then not paid much attention, was taking photographs. This was the White man with the bucket hat who appeared in profile in Mauro's picture and whom I mention on page 207. I had thought that he was one of the humanitarian aid workers who had come from Bujumbura to collect the children at the border. Again with Pierre's help, I was soon able to find his name in the I.C.T.R. archives, and discovered that he had helped with the June 18 convoy from Butare. A few internet searches allowed me to discover that Aldo was an Italian paediatrician posted to Burundi who had decided to join the little team with *Terre des Hommes*. I searched in vain for an e-mail address in order to contact him. The last N.G.O. for which he had worked did not reply to me. There was no trace of him online after 2020; I then wondered whether he had been taken by Covid, which had been responsible for so many deaths in Italy. I was about to throw in the towel when my husband, always a source of good advice, suggested asking my friend Alessandro, the Italian virologist with whom I had once worked for M.S.F. and whom I mention on page 116. Alessandro and his wife Francesca left no stone unturned and finally found Aldo's contact details thanks to the Italian college of medical practitioners. That was how in June I received an emotional message from Alessandro: "Beaaata, we have found Aldo, he is alive!" He told me they had spoken over the telephone, and that although Aldo was very old and had some issues with memory, he clearly remembered our evacuation.

A few days later, when I contacted Aldo myself, he sent me three photographs he had taken on June 18. In one of them I found the young man with Asian features who appeared in three of the pictures taken by the *Terre des Hommes* photographer, and whose identity had until then remained a mystery in my investigation. Fergal Keane had described him in his book as a Japanese photographer. A few months earlier, during an event at the Pompidou Centre library, I had mentioned him to the journalist Colette Braeckman, who had covered the 1994 genocide for the Belgian newspaper *Le Soir*. She had given me the name of the only Japanese journalist who was in the region at the time, and it was that name that I had asked a Japanese colleague of my husband to search for, as I was incapable of finding anything on Japanese websites myself.

What a plot twist it was when Aldo, on being asked whether he remembered the name of the Japanese photographer, said: "The man you can see in the photograph is not Japanese, but Vietnamese." In a few clicks, I had found him: Hiên Lâm Duc, a photographer for the Vu agency. I wrote to him immediately, asking if it was really him in the photograph. That same day I received a laconic reply: "What a surprise. Yes, that's me."

I persevered, explaining the reason for my search, and soon was able to reach him on the telephone. Then again, as chance would have it, he happened to be spending some time in France. Hiên told me with emotion how he had found himself in Butare in June 1994. As a young photographer engaged by a French N.G.O., he had refused to stay comfortably holed up with the other humanitarian aid workers in Bujumbura and had attempted a solo exploratory mission in the south of Rwanda. He had gone as far as Gikongoro with a driver from Zaire to explore locations where his agency might deploy missions as soon as the situation allowed. There were killers all over the roads.

Hiên told me about a scene that had made a deep impression on him. A militiaman posted at a roadblock checked his press I.D. card. He was illiterate and held it upside down. Hiên took a photograph of him. The man, armed to the teeth, got angry and called him a dirty White man. Hiên then had a remarkable survival reaction. He pretended to get angry himself: "How can you call me a White man, you insult me, I'm Yellow!" Hiên went on to say that he had been taking a picture of the banana trees, which reminded him of his home in Asia. That was how he saved himself. He then told me that it was on the return journey that he met Alexis and Deanna in Butare and offered to help them with the evacuations. He drew on his personal memories in his interactions with the children. Born in Laos of Vietnamese parents, he had been a refugee in Thailand before moving to France with his family in the 1970s. In Rwanda, he had played the clown a little, and sung nursery rhymes to make the journey to Burundi less frightening for the children. He was probably the person the children were looking at in the photograph of the truck taken by Tony Wende. Hiên also told me that day that he had archived all of his photographs and spontaneously offered to digitise them and send them to me.

There were 50 of them, in soft black and white. Several were taken in Butare before the departure. I immediately shared them on the group chat that I had created with the children of the convoys back in November 2020, when I had contacted the handful of survivors I knew of on learning that Alexis was dying. Since then, as my investigation progressed, the group had slowly grown. The publication of my book in France accelerated the arrival of other members. A new community was created, allowing everyone to get to know each other (again), and to share their memories. Those who arrived would sometimes ask me to add such and such a friend or cousin who had also been one of the evacuees, and who was living in Kigali or France, the U.S.A. or a small rural town in Rwanda.

With each new meeting, I learn more about every one of their implausible, miraculous journeys. A few days ago, for instance, at the library of Uppsala, during a presentation of my first novel, which has recently been translated into Swedish, I was able to meet Joseph. He was in the June 18 convoy with his young niece and told me that many of the children in Ngoma, his neighbourhood in Butare, had been able to get to the *Terre des Hommes* centre thanks to a righteous Hutu, Laurien Ntezimana, who had managed to drive them safely to the Karubanda social workers' training school. After the genocide, the grown-up children had paid an emotional visit to this man to express their gratitude. Joseph also gave me the contact details of a woman who remembered being one of the little children sitting on my mother and me in the back of the truck, to hide us from the militiamen at the roadblocks. She is now living in Austria.

We are a multitude scattered all over the world.

Two other important events stood out in June 2024.

On June 18, in Kigali, exactly 30 years since our evacuation from Butare, my Belgian-Rwandan writer friend Dominique Celis organised a gathering around *The Convoy*, with the help of Hélène Dumas and thanks to the generous welcome provided by Olivier and Barbara Costa at the Mundi Center, a cultural space opened by the couple in the Rwandan capital. These two people are the elder son and the daughter-in-law of Pierantonio Costa, the Italian consul who had helped Alexis to organise the first convoy. It was therefore in a highly symbolic place that around fifteen children of the convoys gathered that evening, in front of a packed audience, to tell the story of our rescue and to pay homage to those who had organised it. The emotion of the moment was all the more intense because we had learned that very morning that Mariann Costa, Pierantonio's widow, had just passed away in Belgium.

Most of these children were meeting again for the first time in 30 years. For others it was the surprise of finding a former colleague they had worked alongside for years without knowing that they had a common history. We then spent the evening talking together, each of us telling the story of the child we had been in June and July 1994 and of the adult we had become since then. Under the starry sky, those who had become parents listed the symbolic names charged with meanings of renewal and hope that they had given to their children, as victories over death.

While the stories told to the large group aimed to show resilience, in the image of the phoenix country that Rwanda now claims to be, some that were later told to me in the intimacy of face-to-face conversations spoke of more painful journeys. Several of the children had been taken in by their families, who had returned from exile seeking mostly to appropriate the assets of their massacred relatives and who had not always given the young orphans the care and affection they so desperately needed.

The youngest children, the babies taken to *Terre des Hommes* by Hutu who had often picked them up near mass graves, lived with the anxiety of knowing nothing about their origins, and their distress is immeasurable. One of them asked me whether there were any archives that might provide information about where she was found and the identity of the person who had brought her to the Karubanda school in Butare. I could not promise there were, but told her we could take up the investigation again with the organisations that had taken care of the evacuated children.

A survivor of Kaduha also asked me about the children adopted by families in Burundi, who never returned to their country. How could they be found again?

So much remains to be done. I explained that I would need them to be involved in the research I was not able to conduct alone from France. I left Rwanda a few days later, my heart bursting with all the stories I had been told, and with a sense of responsibility that was a little frightening, but also with the hope that this group, which Anne-Marie had said was like a new family, would forge other strong connections.

Finally, on June 30, at the invitation of the *Mémorial de la Shoah*, several protagonists of *The Convoy* came together in

EPILOGUE

Paris. For the first time in 30 years, with four other children, Milan, Delphine, Nadine and Damas, we gathered around Deanna Cavadini, the humanitarian aid worker who had saved us. By our side were two other important witnesses, Fergal Keane and Hiên Lâm Duc.

Before a large audience, we told our stories of those weeks in the midst of the genocide against the Tutsi that marked our lives forever. We paid homage to the courage of a handful of men and women who had remained anonymous until now, those who had organised the convoys to life.

As I am writing these words, our chat group has gathered together 45 children of the convoys. Others will undoubtedly arrive. Several of them have told me about their plans to write a book. I know that there are many more images to find, much more information to track down in the archives. I still have not been able to find the photograph published by the magazine *No Limits*. But I also know that I am no longer alone in my quest, that we will continue to write this story together, carried forward by the "solidarity of the shaken".

Several Western journalists have told me how much this book has unsettled them in the way they see the world, how much it has made them reflect on their relationship to storytelling and their work. One of these is a journalist who has been working in Africa for several decades, who told me that since reading the book she always takes a Polaroid camera with her when reporting and routinely gives the people she interviews a copy of the photograph she has taken of them.

In the eight months since the publication of *The Convoy* in France, I have been overwhelmed by a maelstrom of emotions, but the one which has dominated has been a profound sense of gratitude. Towards all those men and women who have read and shared the book, towards all those people who have participated in the chain of transmission of information. Gratitude finally for literature, which has allowed me to gather together the children of the convoys, our multitude scattered throughout the world.

Bordeaux, September 15, 2024

Notes

1 Initially published by La Cheminante in 2015, the work was republished in the collection *Ejo, suivi de Lézardes et autres nouvelles* (Ejo, followed by cracks and other stories) by Autrement. This consists of thirty short stories and was the winner of several literary prizes.
2 Ibuka France – Mémoire, Justice et Soutien aux rescapés (Ibuka France – memory, justice and survivor support) is an organisation founded in 2002 whose objectives are to preserve the memory of the genocide against the Tutsi in Rwanda, and provide justice and support for the survivors in France. The first Ibuka N.G.O. was founded in August 1994 in Belgium. Other branches followed, in Rwanda, Italy, the Netherlands, Switzerland.
3 Nickname that the Hutu militia gave itself.
4 See the map pages 10–11.
5 The Arusha Accords, signed in several stages, between July 1992 and August 1993.
6 This name has been changed.
7 On June 27, 1994, a group of French soldiers of the *Opération Turquoise* discovered around 2,000 Tutsi survivors who were still under threat at Bisesero. The soldiers promised to return to help them as soon as possible. It would take three days for another battalion to find them again, under pressure from journalists. In the meantime, the Hutu killers, who then knew where they were, had killed half the Tutsi inhabitants of Bisesero.
8 *Radio Télévision Libre des Mille Collines*, later nicknamed "Radio Machete", was the first private radio station, created in 1993, and one of the principal propaganda tools in anti-Tutsi hate deployed by the dignitaries of "Hutu Power", the extremist Hutu ideology.
9 The International Residual Mechanism for Criminal Tribunals is an organisation whose aim is to preserve the heritage of the two

international criminal tribunals, one for Rwanda, which closed in 2015, and the other for the former Yugoslavia, which ceased its activities in 2017.

10 I have not managed to ascertain whether there were one or two convoys at the beginning of June. The accounts written by Alexis to which I was able to get access in the archives of *Terre des Hommes* mention two convoys: the one on June 5 was completed without any great difficulty, whereas the one the next day is presented as a real nightmare. But during his deposition at the International Criminal Tribunal for Rwanda in 2007, Alexis revises his first statements and speaks only of a single convoy, on June 5, which was said to be particularly difficult. This is the one I am relating here. I became aware of this discrepancy after Alexis's death and no-one else among those whom I questioned later has been able to give concrete information about these events.

11 This name has been changed.

12 This name has been changed.

13 This name has also been changed.

Chronology

Chronology of the history of the genocide against the Tutsi established by Hélène Dumas (*Centre National de la Recherche Scientifique*)

1897 Establishment of a military protectorate by Germany on Rwanda.
1990 Founding of the first Catholic mission at Save by priests belonging to the Society of African Missions.
1916 Belgian troops drive out the few German officers and the country passes under Belgian military administration.
1922 Belgium receives the mandate from the League of Nations over the "Territories of Ruanda-Urundi".
1931 Identity cards include the indication of ethnicity, with the objective of a census of able-bodied adult men for tax collection purposes and to impose forced labour. King Musinga, hostile to evangelisation, is deposed by the Belgian authorities. His son, Mutara Rudahigwa, accedes to the throne.
1946 Rwanda and Burundi pass into Belgian control, the United Nations having taken over from the League of Nations.
1957 Publication of the *Bahutu Manifesto*, subtitled *Note on the social aspect of the native racial problem in Rwanda*, signed by individuals of the Hutu elite of which Grégoire Kayibanda was a member. This text recommends keeping the mention of ethnicity on identity cards and advises the use of medicine in cases of "interbreeding".
1959 (September) Creation of the nationalist party, *Union Nationale Rwandaise*, composed primarily of Tutsi high chiefs placed in their positions by the Belgian colonisers. They call for the country's independence.
(October) Grégoire Kayibanda founds the *Parti du Mouvement et de l'Émancipation Hutu* (Parmehutu, the Party of the Hutu Emancipation Movement) which demands the abolition of "Tutsi colonisation" before the departure of the Belgians.

(November) The "Hutu social revolution" leads to the massacre of several hundred Tutsi. The violence is aimed primarily at the members of the "native" administration, in other words the chiefs and under-chiefs, put in place by the coloniser who thus reverses the initial alliance by encouraging the "Hutu Revolution". Tens of thousands of Tutsi go into exile in the bordering countries.

1961 The monarchy is abolished by referendum.

1962 (1 July) Rwanda gains independence, Grégoire Kayibanda becomes president.

1963–4 (December–January) Incursions by Tutsi exiles (nicknamed *Inyenzi* – cockroaches – because of their nocturnal attacks) from the south of the country lead to fierce repression of local Tutsi. The massacres gain considerable scope in Gikongoro: between 10 and 20 per cent of the Tutsi population of that prefecture are assassinated by groups armed with lances and sticks, on the order of the *préfet*. The violence then spreads to the neighbouring prefectures, causing between 10,000 and 14,000 deaths. In the issue of *Le Monde*, dated February 6, 1964, the philosopher Bertrand Russel denounces "the most horrible and systematic massacre we have had occasion to witness since the extermination of the Jews by the Nazis in Europe". Tens of thousands of Tutsi join the growing ranks of refugees.

1973 (February–March) Purges organised by "Committees for Public Safety" provoke new violence against the Tutsi, who are driven out of schools, universities, seminaries and the public service. Homes are burned and around 200 people assassinated.

(July 5) Major-General Juvénal Habyarimana, a Hutu officer from the north of Rwanda, takes power after a coup. He intends to re-establish order and national unity.

1975 The *Mouvement Révolutionnaire National pour le Développement* (M.R.N.D.) is founded. It is the only authorised political party in the country.

1987 Faced with the Habyarimana regime's refusal to recognise the right of Tutsi refugees to return, they – and their descendants – found the Rwandan Patriotic Front (R.P.F.). This movement forms an armed branch, the Rwandan Patriotic Army (R.P.A.). It also includes Hutu dissidents opposed to the established power in Kigali.

CHRONOLOGY

1988–9   Rwanda is faced with a serious economic crisis following the collapse of the prices of coffee and tea on the world market.

1990   (October 1) The R.P.F. launches its first offensive in the east of the country, which is quickly controlled by the Rwandan Armed Forces, supported by troops from Zaire, Belgium and France, in particular. In reaction, the Rwandan authorities throw several thousand people in prison, of whom the majority are Tutsi, accused of "complicity" with the enemy.

1991   (February) The R.P.F. takes one of the main cities of the north of the country, Ruhengeri, and liberates its prisoners. The attacks by the R.P.F. are used as a pretext for the massacre of the Bagogwe Tutsi from the region of Kibilira: nearly 600 people are assassinated in this region in the space of one year.

(June) Faced with widespread protest from civil society, President Habyarimana concedes and allows multiple parties, which are then authorised by the new constitution. Several opposition organisations are created.

1992   The *Interahamwe* militias, a movement of young people affiliated with the M.R.N.D., are created. They violently display their support for the presidential party several times during the year. Those militias are joined in their fight against "the Tutsi enemy" by a racist party, the Coalition for the Defence of the Republic (C.D.R.).

(March) The broadcast on national radio of a tract wrongly attributing the assassination of Hutu to members of a predominantly Tutsi party is used as a pretext to set off massacres in the region of Bugesera (south of Kigali). Militiamen, local authorities and civilians join forces to effect this.

1993   (August) The Arusha Peace Accords are signed between President Habyarimana, the opposition parties and the R.P.F. They entail the sharing of power and the merging of the armies.

(October) The United Nations Assistance Mission for Rwanda (U.N.A.M.I.R.) commanded by the Canadian general Roméo Dallaire starts its deployment. It is composed of 2,500 men.

1994   (April) In the evening of April 6, the aircraft carrying President Habyarimana is shot down. The elite units of the Rwandan army and militias lock down Kigali. Colonel Bagosara calls a crisis committee in which he refuses to invest power in Prime Minister Agathe Uwilingiyimana as the Constitution requires.

(April 7) The prime minister is assassinated at her residence by members of the military; Hutu political opponents are systematically eliminated. The ten Blue Helmets from the U.N. peacekeeping force detailed to the protection of the prime minister are massacred at Camp Kigali by Rwandan soldiers.

(April 8–9) An interim government is constituted and sworn in. Respecting the facade of the Arusha Accords, it brings together politicians from different parties but all belonging to the "Hutu Power" faction, i.e. the extremist fringe. The government relays extermination orders to local administrations. The R.P.F. takes the offensive once again.

(April 9–15) Several Western powers, including Belgium and France, send troops to Rwanda to ensure the evacuation of their citizens. The soldiers do not intervene at all to bring the massacres to an end.

(April 11) The Belgian military in the U.N.A.M.I.R. depart from the Official Technical School in Kicukiro, abandoning thousands of Tutsi refugees to certain death. 5,000 of them are assassinated in a mass extermination that very evening on the hill of Nyanza-Kicukiro.

(April 21) The United Nations Security Council reduces the numbers of the U.N. force from 2,500 to 270 men, most of whom are civilians.

(May) The majority of victims have by now been assassinated.

(June 22) France launches *Opération Turquoise* under the aegis of the United Nations. When the genocide has already been committed, the French forces create a buffer zone in the west of the country allowing the officials from the extremist government to flee to Zaire from the advancing troops of the R.P.F.

(July 4) The R.P.F. wins the battle of Kigali.

(July 19) The forces of the genocide are routed, having pushed more than two million Hutu civilians into exile in Zaire and Tanzania. A new government for "national unity" is established in Kigali, dominated by the R.P.F.

Acknowledgements

I wish to thank here the people whose support and collaboration have allowed me to carry out my investigation and write this book, those who agreed to share their memories, allowed me to cite their writings, gave me access to documents, passed on contacts, opened a door.

Muriel Blanc, Barbara Boyle-Saidi, Bertille Descamps, Alice Doyard, Mark Doyle, Bénédicte Gilardi, Rizwana Hamid, Jean-Luc Imhof, Fergal Keane, Jacques Morel, Nathan Réra, Alessandro Soria, Tony Wende and Ariane Zwahlen.

Dominique Celis and Hélène Dumas for the solid bonds of friendship between here and there.

Infinite thanks to Deanna Cavadini and Alexis Briquet – who is unfortunately no longer with us – for their fine humanity, their generosity, their courage. Thank you for our saved lives.

To Aldo Bordigoni, Hiên Lâm Duc, Patrizia Miazzo and Mauro Parmesani, for their work alongside Deanna and Alexis on June 18, 1994, and for the photographs.

A thousand thanks to the other children of the convoys, who are now upstanding women and men, *bavandimwe twarokokanye*, for their confidence, their precious memories and their encouragement: Damas Dukundane, Rodrigue Iradukunda, Annick Kayitesi-Jozan, Manzi Rugirangoga, Delphine Umuhoza, Claire Umutoni, Willy Wasungu.

Thank you to the children of Pierantonio Costa and the team of the *Mémorial de la Shoah* who enabled us to find each other in Kigali and Paris, thirty years later.

To Claire Fercak, my editor, for the road travelled together.

To Yann, always, immensely.

Sources

Costa, Pierantonio and Luciano Scalettari, *La Lista del Console* (The consul's list), Edizioni Paoline, 2004.

Delbo, Charlotte, *Auschwitz and After*, translated by Rosette C. Lamont, Yale University Press, 1985.

Delbo, Charlotte, *Convoy to Auschwitz*, translated by Carol Cosman, Northeastern University Press, 1997.

Didi-Huberman, Georges, *Bark*, translated by Samuel Martin, MIT Press, 2017.

Dumas, Hélène, *Le Génocide au village* (Genocide in the village), Seuil, 2014.

Dumas, Hélène, *Beyond Despair: The Rwanda Genocide against the Tutsi through the Eyes of Children*, translated by Catherine Porter, Fordham University Press, 2024.

Duras, Marguerite, *War: A Memoir*, translated by Barbara Bray, Collins, 1986.

Gurnah, Abdulrazak, *By the Sea*, Bloomsbury, 2002.

Kabarari, Valens, *Basculement, Rwanda 94* (Tipping point, Rwanda 94), Edilivre, 2019.

Kayitesi-Jozan, Annick, *Nous existons encore* (We are still alive), Michel Lafon, 2004.

Kayitesi-Jozan, Annick, *Même Dieu ne veut pas s'en mêler* (Even God doesn't want to get involved), Seuil, 2017.

Keane, Fergal, *Season of Blood, a Rwandan Journey*, Viking, 1995.

Lorde, Audre, "A Litany for Survival", in *The Black Unicorn*, Penguin Classics, 2019.

Lyamukuru, Félicité (in collaboration with Nathalie Caprioli), *L'Ouragan a frappé Nyundo* (The hurricane struck Nyundo), Éditions Cerisier, 2018.

Mujawayo, Esther (with Saouâd Belhaddad), *SurVivantes*, Éditions de l'Aube, 2004.

SOURCES

Nachtwey, James, *Inferno*, Phaidon, 1999.

Piton, Florent, *Le Génocide des Tutsi du Rwanda* (The genocide of the Tutsi of Rwanda), La Découverte, 2014.

Réra, Nathan, "Rwanda, images du désastre, du temps de l'information au temps de la mémoire" (Rwanda, images of the disaster, from the time of information to the time of memory), in Arts & Sociétés, Lettre du séminaire no. 61, Sciences Po, s.d., https://www.sciencespo.fr/artsetsocietes/fr/archives/1192#_ftn8.

Réra, Nathan, *Rwanda, entre crise morale et malaise esthétique – Les médias, la photographie et le cinéma à l'épreuve du génocide des Tutsi (1994–2014)* (Rwanda, between moral crisis and aesthetic malaise: The media, photography and film faced with the genocide of the Tutsi (1994–2014)), Les Presses du réel, 2014.

Roth, Philip, "Conversation in Turin with Primo Levi", in *Shop Talk*, Vintage, 2002.

Rugirangoga, Manzi, *La Légende de Havilah* (The legend of Havilah), Éditions Elimu, 2022.

Rurangwa, Révérien, *Génocidé* (Genocided), Presses de la Renaissance, 2006.

Salgado, Sebastião, *Exodus*, Taschen, 2016.

Sebald, W.G., *Austerlitz*, translated by Anthea Bell, Hamish Hamilton, 2001.

Sontag, Susan, *Regarding the Pain of Others*, Penguin Books, 2004.

Suau, Anthony and Florence Aubenas, *On a deux yeux de trop. Avec les réfugiés rwandais, Goma, Zaire, 1994* (We have two eyes too many. With the Rwandan refugees, Goma, Zaire, 1994), Actes Sud, 1995.

Umubyeyi Mairesse, Beata, *Ejo, suivi de lézardes et autres nouvelles* (Ejo, followed by cracks and other stories), Autrement, 2020.

Umubyeyi Mairesse, Beata, *All Your Children, Scattered*, translated by Alison Anderson, Europa Editions, 2022.

Wende, Hamilton, *Deadline from the Edge: Images of War – Congo to Afghanistan*, Penguin Books (South Africa), 2003 (then self-published 2019).

Wende, Hamilton, *True North: African Roads Less Travelled*, William Waterman Publications, 1995 (then self-published 2019).

Wieviorka, Annette, *L'Heure d'exactitude – Histoire, mémoire, témoignage. Entretiens avec Séverine Nikel* (The hour of exactitude – history, memory, testimony. Interviews with Séverine Nikel), Albin Michel, 2011.

https://francegenocidetutsi.org/exhd460bfr.pdf
https://francegenocidetutsi.org/index.html.en
https://mg.co.za/article/2011-08-05-murder-and-memory-in-rwanda/
https://nolimits.com/en/history/
https://www.jamesnachtwey.com/
https://www.sentinelles.org/en/
https://www.tdh.org/en

Index

A
Action against Hunger N.G.O. 256
Aides 42
A.I.D.S./H.I.V. 42, 116–7, 142, 148
Aldo (Italian aid worker) 262–3
All Your Children, Scattered (B. Umubyeyi Mairesse) 242
Allied/D-Day landings 50th anniversary, Normandy 93
ancestry, Rwandan shared 70
Anselme, Robert 63
apartheid 48, 93
Appelfeld, Aaron 25
Armenian genocide 67, 229
Askolovitch, Evelyn 35–6, 99
assassination of President Habyarimana 78–9
Auschwitz-Birkenau concentration camp 61, 90

B
"Basculement, Rwanda 94" play 37
B.B.C. (British Broadcasting Corporation)
  "Fergal Keane: Living with P.T.S.D." documentary 215–6
  Genocide against the Tutsi/convoy coverage 13, 31, 42–52, 53–5, 125, 131–5, 180–1, 193, 209, 215–7, 252–3, 260–1
  interviews with *préfet* Nsabimana 51–2, 133, 181–4, 200, 252–3
  see also Hamid, Rizwana "Rizu"; Harrison, David; Keane, Fergal; Middleton, Glenn; Wende, Tony

Belgian international school, Butare 67–8, 103–4, 123
Belgian occupation of Rwanda 70, 84
Belgian para-commandos 80, 243, 245
Belgian Red Cross 156, 167–8, 179, 189
  see also Groupe Scolaire, Butare
Benaco refugee camp, Tanzania 248
Birara, Aminadabu 111
Blanc, Muriel 75
Blondelle, Chantal and Bernard 130
Bouju, Jean-Marc 249
Braeckman, Colette 262
Briquet, Alexis 139–40, 142, 149–55, 157, 159–72, 177, 179–81, 185, 188–9, 191–3, 211–3, 218–9, 224–5, 256, 260, 264
Brothers of Charity 162
Bujumbura city and refugee reception centre, Burundi 129–30, 155, 169–70, 179, 189–90, 195, 209–10, 213, 226, 235, 256–7, 260, 263
Bukavu refugee camps, Zaire 161, 163, 177, 188–9
Burundi/Rwanda border 13, 21, 31, 43, 52, 55, 58–9, 128–9, 133–5, 151, 169–70, 172, 184, 206–7, 261
  see also Bujumbura city and refugee reception centre, Burundi

Butare, Rwanda 22, 37, 45, 50–2, 78, 80–1, 89, 140, 154, 161–2, 172, 188–9, 210–1, 213–4, 229, 259, 263–5
  see also B.B.C.; home and refuge in Butare hotel complex, author's; *Groupe Scolaire*, Butare; Karubanda school, Butare; Nsabimana, *préfet* Sylvain; *Terre des Hommes*
"Butare Six" I.C.T.R. trials 192–4

C
Calais, Christophe 249–50
Cambodian genocide 67, 241
Cameroon 142
captioning genocide photographs, misrepresentation in 201–2, 239, 244, 246, 249, 251–2
Carbonare, Jean 244
Cavadini, Deanna 151, 153, 157–9, 179–81, 189, 203, 264, 267
Cavaliere del Lavoro Filippo Giardello 254–5
Celis, Dominique 265
Chirac, Jacques 63
cholera epidemic, Zaire refugee camp 247–9
Chrétien, Jean-Pierre 261
Christine, Sister 79, 105, 117, 119–20, 130, 185
colonialism 18, 69–70, 84
the convoys *see Terre des Hommes*
Copeland, Richard 130
Cordess, Alexis 250
Costa, Mariann 265
Costa, Olivier and Barbara 265
Costa, Pierantonio 142, 159–72, 178–9, 211, 257, 265
COVID-19 global pandemic 144
Culbuter le malheur (B. Umubyeyi Mairesse) 260
Ćurić, Vjekoslav 170–1, 180

D
de Dieu Rwamihare, Jean "Bonhomme" 36–7
de Gaulle, Charles 63–4
Delahaye, Luc 197, 245–6, 250
Delbo, Charlotte 25, 73, 97
Democratic Republic of Congo (D.R.C.) *see* Zaire
Descamps, Bertille 144
Desforges, Alison 141
Didi-Huberman, Georges 65
Doyard, Alice 215–6
Doyle, Mark 42–5
Dukundane, Damas 223–8, 234–6, 267
Dumas, Hélène 186–7, 194–5, 223, 225, 236, 259, 261, 265
Duras, Marguerite 63

E
Ejo (B. Umubyeyi Mairesse) 21
ethnicity and colonialism, Rwandan 69–70
Euthymia convent, Kaduha 186
evacuation of foreign nationals from Rwanda 80–1, 118, 127, 148, 159, 163, 232, 245

F
Federal Office for Foreigners, Swiss 146
fiction writing, author's 21–4, 242, 260
F.I.F.A. World Cup (1994) 51
foreign military forces in Rwanda 80, 93, 127, 243, 245
  see also United Nations
France
  author's life post-evacuation 16–9, 130
  censored media coverage of Genocide against the Tutsi 245–6, 248–50

INDEX

government support for Hutu
  powers 93, 103, 106, 134, 141,
  188, 246
Opération Turquoise, French 111,
  119, 188, 190, 247, 249–50

G

Gaillard, Philippe 140, 151
Gatagara centre for handicapped
  children, Rwanda 162, 226
Genocide Memorial, Gisozi 229
Genocide against the Tutsi 17–9,
  48–52
  begins in Kigali 78–9
  deliberate transmission of
    A.I.D.S./H.I.V. 116–7
  failure of foreign powers 127, 245
  fate of Hutu allied with Tutsi
    109–10
  Holocaust parallels 62–7
  Hutu attack children's refuge,
    Groupe Scolaire, Butare 168
  Hutu genocidal government and
    army 47–52, 78, 91, 119, 124,
    131, 134, 160–3, 166, 168–9,
    187–8, 245
  French government support for
    93, 103, 106, 134, 141,
    188, 246
  Ibuka Rwanda archives 236–7
  impossibility/futility of self-
    defence 110–2
  Kaduha massacres 186–7, 224–5
  Kigali massacres 37, 50, 78–9,
    123, 127, 148, 168, 210–1,
    246
  lack of global recognition/
    acknowledgement 63–5
  murders begin in Butare 89–90
  Nyarubuye massacres 49–50
  rape victims 113–7, 122
  representation in Western
    media 199–202, 238–51,
    252–3

  roadblock/border militiamen 44,
    47–8, 70, 119, 125, 132, 171–2,
    181, 183–4, 263
  Tutsi orphans targeted 131
  Tutsi resistance in Bisesero hills
    111–2
  see also B.B.C.; home and refuge
    in Butare hotel complex,
    author's; Nsabimana, *préfet*
    Sylvain; rescue and escape from
    Butare, author's; Rwandan
    Patriotic Front /Tutsi forces;
    Terre des Hommes; Tutsi
    population, Rwanda
Gilardi, Bénédicte 75
Gisozi Genocide memorial, Kigali
  71, 140–1
Givord, Aymeric 139
Goma, Zaire 134, 188
Great Depression, USA 251
Groupe Scolaire, Butare 156,
  162, 167–72, 211–2
Gurnah, Abdulrazak 228

H

Habyarimana, President 78–9
Hamid, Rizwana "Rizu" 48, 50,
  131, 132–3, 134, 216
Harrison, David 47–50, 131, 134
Holocaust 15, 20, 35–6, 62–5, 90
  Kindertransport 65–6
  Sonderkommando photographs
    61–2
home and refuge in Butare hotel
  complex, author's 79–82
  discovered by the Hutu militia
    96–7, 100–8
  in hiding at the hotel 82–3
  author's mother's deterioration
    89, 91–2
  experiencing the violence outside
    88–9
  food supplies 87–9, 94–5
  living in the basement 85–7

near discoveries 83, 85, 91
news of genocide from hotel staff 88–90
radio reports 93–4
hotel gardener and father 83, 88, 100, 109
Hutu officers at the hotel 83–5
Karoli (hotel cook) 82, 87–8, 90, 94–5, 100, 113, 258–9
threatened rape 113–5
Vénuste (hotel waiter) 82–4, 115
see also rescue and escape from Butare; *Terre des Hommes*
Horizon "Fergal Keane: Living with P.T.S.D." B.B.C. documentary 215 *see also* B.B.C.
host family in France, author's 19, 130
humanitarian work, author's 19–20, 42, 115–6, 141–2
Hutu and Tutsi shared ancestry 70
Hutu genocidal government and army 47–52, 78, 91, 119, 124, 131, 134, 160–3, 166, 168–9, 187–8, 245
French support 93, 103, 106, 134, 141, 188, 246
roadblock/border militia 44, 47–8, 70, 119, 125, 132, 171–2, 181, 183–4, 263
see also Genocide against the Tutsi; International Criminal Tribunal for Rwanda; Nsabimana, *préfet* Sylvain; Nteziryayo, Colonel Alphonse
Hutu refugees 119, 134, 166, 171, 188, 190, 230, 246–9

I
I Am Fifteen – And I Do not Want to Die (C. Arnothy) 68
Ibuka Belgique 36
Ibuka France 36, 77, 174

Ibuka Rwanda archivists 236–7
I.D. cards and ethnicity, Rwandan 70, 82–3, 102, 183–5
Imhof, Jean-Luc 232
Inkotanyi rebels *see* Rwandan Patriotic Front /Tutsi forces
Interahamwe militiamen 47–9, 131–2
see also Hutu genocidal government
International Committee of the Red Cross (I.C.R.C.) 140–2, 151–3, 161, 163, 168–70, 172, 174, 176–9, 189, 257
see also Red Cross
International Criminal Tribunal for Rwanda (I.C.T.R.) 26, 45, 46, 51, 117, 139, 163, 180–2, 191–4, 230–1
International Federation for Human Rights (I.F.H.R.) 244
international school, Butare 67–8, 103–4, 123

J
Jaar, Alfredo 250
Jan Michalski Foundation 76
journalistic perspective of Genocide against the Tutsi, Western 199–202, 238–53

K
Kaddish for an Unborn Child (I. Kertész) 41
Kaduha massacres 186–7, 223–5
survivors 194–5, 223–5, 234–5, 266
Kaiser, Edmond 146–7, 159
Kanyabashi, Joseph 192, 230–1
Karenzi (university professor) 89
Karoli (hotel cook) 82, 87–8, 90, 94–5, 100, 113, 258–9
Karubanda school, Butare 118–24, 154, 172, 179–81, 206, 211–3, 234, 265

INDEX

Kayanza Red Cross refugee camp, Burundi 172–3
Kayitesi-Jozan, Annick 26, 41, 154–5
Keane, Fergal 44–51, 53–4, 130–5, 150, 191–3, 215–16, 237, 252–3, 262, 267
Keats, John 50
Kertész, Imre 29, 41, 63
Khmer Rouge 67, 241
Kigali massacres 37, 50, 78–9, 123, 127, 148, 168, 210–11, 246
  Genocide memorial 71, 140–1
  see also Genocide against the Tutsi
Kindertransport, Second World War 65–6
Kösser, Sister Milgitha 186–7, 223–5, 235

L
La Lista del Console documentary (2004) 178
Lâm Duc, Hiên 263–4, 267
Lange, Dorothea 251
Langfus, Anna 63
Le Monde 250
Le Soir 262
Leave None to Tell the Story: Genocide in Rwanda (A. Desforges) 141
Levi, Primo 25, 63
Liberal Party, Rwandan 123
Libération 249
Lorde, Audre 24
Lyamukuru, Félicité 36–7
Lycée Beaucamps-Ligny, France 19
Lycée Thierry-Maulnier, France (now *Lycée Mélinée et Missak Manouchian*) 35–6, 75–6, 99

M
Mairesse (author's husband), Yann 20–1, 42–3, 47, 54, 56, 119, 139, 175–6, 206, 215, 262

Mandela, Nelson 48, 93
Médecins sans Frontières (M.S.F.) N.G.O. 115–6, 141–2
Mémorial de la Shoah, Paris 65, 76–7, 174, 237, 266–7
Memory Week, Lycée *Thierry-Maulnier* 35–6
Mendelsohn, Daniel 29, 195
Miazzo, Patrizia 179, 203, 208, 252, 253
Middleton, Glenn 44, 49–50, 131–2, 134, 208, 217
"Migrant Mother" photograph (D. Lange) 251–2
Mille Collines radio station 148
Ministry for National Unity and Civic Engagement, Rwanda 237
Ministry of Social Affairs, Rwanda 142
Mitterrand, François 93, 106
Morel, Jacques 139, 174
Morrison, Toni 21
Muhabura radio 93–4
Mujawayo, Esther 137
multiracial elections, South Africa 48
Munyengango, Colonel François 169, 171–2, 177, 191–2

N
Nachtwey, James 248–9
Nairobi 134
Ndagijimana/Rugirangoga, Manzi Cédric 155–7
Ndasingwa, Landoald 123
Ndayambaje, Élie 192
Ndera psychiatric hospital, Rwanda 245
Ndore, Frank 133–4
No Limits magazine 254–5
Nsabimana, *préfet* Sylvain 45, 51–2, 54–5, 130–4, 169–71, 181–5, 189, 191–3, 200, 224–5, 252–3
Ntahobari, Arsène Shalom 192
Ntezimana, Laurien 264–5

Nteziryayo, Colonel Alphonse 126, 130, 182, 192
Nyanza-Kicukiro massacre 246
Nyanza orphanage, Rwanda 164–7
Nyiramasuhuko, Pauline 51, 192

O
Opération Turquoise, French 111, 119, 188, 190, 247, 249–50
orphans targeted, Tutsi 131
Owens Thompson, Florence 251–2

P
Panorama B.B.C. documentary 46, 53–5, 181, 200, 252–3
see also B.B.C.
Papon, Maurice 63
parenthood after genocide 41–2
Parmesani, Mauro 179, 200–1, 203–9, 219–20, 231, 236, 239, 252–3, 259, 261
Peress, Gilles 248, 250
Philippin, Daniel 169–70, 257
photographs and film of *Terre des Hommes* convoys
  Aldo (Italian aid worker) 262–3
  author identifies her mother and herself 209, 261
  Hiên Lâm Duc 263–4, 267
  Mauro Parmesani 200–1, 203–9, 215, 219–20, 231, 236, 239, 253, 259, 261
  sharing with survivors 28, 37–40, 65, 142–3, 195, 209–10, 231, 234–6, 258–9, 264–5
  Terre des Hommes archives in Switzerland 144–6, 219–22, 232–5
  tracking and uncovering the B.B.C. archive records 13, 31, 37, 42–8, 53–60, 180–4, 215–18, 236, 260–1
  see also Umubyeyi Mairesse, Beata

photographs in Rwandan culture 68–71
Pigeot, François 107, 117–9
Piton, Florence 127
Pocar, Fausto 194
Poe, Edgar Allan 84
pogroms in the '50, '60s and '70s, Tutsi 48, 110, 129, 134
Pol Pot 241
post-traumatic stress disorder 215–6
presidential guards (P.G.), Hutu 115
psychotherapy 19
Pull, Brenda 226–8
Pull, William M. 225–8, 239
"Purloined Letter" (E.A. Poe) 84

R
Radio Burundi 103
Radio France Internationale 93, 103
radio reports, global 93–5, 103
Radio Rwanda 103
Radio Télévision Suisse (R.T.S.) 146, 167
Rafiki (author's cousin) 78, 95, 129–30, 223
rape victims 113–7, 122
Red Crescent Society 174
Red Cross 168, 171–2, 175–80, 211
  Belgian 156, 167–8, 179, 189
  see also International Committee of the Red Cross
refugee camps, Zaire 134, 142, 161, 163–4, 177, 189, 213, 247–9
  see also Hutu refugees; *Opération Turquoise;* Tutsi population, Rwandan
religious orders, Rwandan Tutsi helped by 79, 81, 105, 117–20, 129–30, 141, 162, 164–7, 170–2, 180, 185–7, 223–4
  see also Karubanda school, Butare; Nyanza orphanage, Rwanda

INDEX

Rencontres du Livre Francophone 223
Réra, Nathan 241, 245–50
rescue and escape from Butare, author's
  border encounter with *préfet* Nsabimana 128
  at Bujumbura refugee reception centre, Burundi 129–30
  help from François Pigeot 117–20
  at the Karubanda school, Butare 119–24
  mother held at gunpoint at Burundi border crossing 44, 47, 126–7
  recollection of convoy journey 56, 124–5
  separated and reunited with mother in Butare 117, 121
  see also Terre des Hommes
Resistance, French 63
roadblock/border militia 44, 47–8, 70, 119, 125, 132, 171–2, 181, 183–4, 263
Robert, Patrick 245
Rodolphe (aid worker) 256–7
Rodrigue (actor and convoy survivor) 37–9, 156
Roma genocides 67
Roosevelt, Franklin D. 251
Royo, Carlos 149
Rurangwa, Révérien 146
Rutayisire, Faustin 212
Rwakayonza, Pierre 211
Rwandan Patriotic Front (R.P.F.)/ Tutsi forces 48–50, 78, 93–4, 134, 149, 167, 188, 190–1
Rybinski, Gauthier 248

S
Salgado, Sebastião 248
Sarr, Mohamed Mbougar 229
Sebald, W.G. 33, 66

Seine, Michel 174–7
Seko, Mobutu Sese 134
self-defence, impossibility/futility of 110–12
Sentinelles N.G.O. 146–8
Seventh-day Adventist Church 141
"The Shadow of War" exhibition, *Maison européenne de la photographie*, Paris 248–9
Shoah Memorial, Paris 65, 76–7, 174, 237
"silence of survivors" 63–4
Sonderkommando 61–2
Sontag, Susan 240
South Africa 48, 93
Suau, Anthony 248
Sunnier family 164, 172, 211
  see also Umutoni, Claire "Fifi"

T
Terre des Hommes (A. de Saint-Exupéry) 16
Terre des Hommes N.G.O. 13, 16, 31, 37, 76–7, 119, 121, 128–30, 141, 146–7, 179
  Alexis Briquet 139–40, 145, 149–55, 157, 159–72, 177, 179–81, 185, 188, 191–2, 211–3, 218–19, 224–5, 256, 260, 264
  the archives in Switzerland 144–6, 219–22, 232–5
  the children from Kaduha 187, 194–5, 223–5, 234–5, 266
  the convoys
    first convoy: from *Groupe Scolaire*, Butare (6 June) 168–72, 211–2, 257
    second convoy: from Karubanda school, Butare (18 June) 180–5, 230–1, 259, 262, 264–5
    author's recollection of the journey 56, 124–5

third convoy: from Karubanda
school, Butare (3 July)
187–90, 257–9
Fergal Keane's recollections
130–5
information from Michel Seine
176–8
préfet Sylvian Nsabimana 51–2,
54–5, 128, 169–71, 181–5,
189–90, 193
procurement of vehicles 170–1,
189
correspondence with the Hutu
Rwandan Government 160–3,
169
expulsion from Rwanda by the
Tutsi government 190–1
Nyanza orphanage rescue 164–7
photographs and film of the
convoys
Aldo (Italian aid worker) 262–3
author identifies her mother and
herself 209, 261
Hiên Lâm Duc 263–4, 267
Mauro Parmesani 200–1,
203–9, 215, 219–20, 231,
236, 239, 253, 259, 261
sharing with survivors 28,
37–40, 65, 142–3, 195,
209–10, 231, 234–6, 258–9,
264–5
Terre des Hommes archives in
Switzerland 144–6, 219–22,
232–5
tracking and uncovering the
B.B.C. archive records 13,
31, 37, 42–8, 53–60, 180–4,
215–18, 236, 260–1
Red Cross help withdrawn
169–70, 177–8, 180
see also Bujumbura refugee
reception camp, Burundi;
Groupe Scolaire, Butare;
Karubanda school, Butare;
photographs and film of *Terre
des Hommes* convoys; religious
orders, Rwandan Tutsi helped
by; Umubyeyi Mairesse,
Beata
Time Magazine 249
Tutsi population, Rwandan
conquering government 190–1
fate of allied Hutu 109–10
and Hutu shared ancestry 70
Nyarubuye Church massacre
49–50
pogroms in the '50s, '60s and
'70s 48, 110, 129, 134
refugees 45, 48–9, 156, 168,
171–2, 176–7, 189, 193, 212,
230, 245
see also B.B.C.; Bujumbura city
and refugee reception centre,
Burundi; Genocide against
the Tutsi; *Groupe Scolaire,*
Butare; Kaduha massacres;
Karubanda school, Butare;
Nyanza orphanage, Rwanda;
religious orders, Rwandan Tutsi
helped by; Rwandan Patriotic
Front (R.P.F.)/Tutsi forces; *Terre
des Hommes*; Beata Umubyeyi
Mairesse, Beata
Twa ancestry 70

U
ubwoko 69–70
Uganda, Tutsi refugees in 48–9
Umubyeyi, Joseline 230
Umubyeyi Mairesse, Beata 13,
15–9
anxieties about telling this story
23–7
approach to writing this story
28–30, 98–9
contact with Alexis Briquet
149–55, 157, 185, 188–9, 200,
218–9

INDEX

contact with fellow escapees 37–9, 142–3, 153–7, 195, 209–14, 223–31, 234–6, 258–61, 264–8
"Fergal Keane: Living with P.T.S.D." B.B.C. documentary 215–6
fiction writing 21–4, 242
finding images of self and mother in the convoy 209, 261
French Higher Education, Sorbonne 141
in hiding at the hotel complex, Butare 79–82
    discovered by the Hutu militia 96–7, 100–8
    experiencing the violence outside 88–9
    first encounter with Hutu forces 81–2
    food supplies 87–9, 94–5
    global radio reports 93–4
    helping a Tutsi stranger 80
    hotel gardener and father 83, 88, 100, 109
    Hutu officers at the hotel 83–5
    Karoli (hotel cook) 82, 87–90, 94–5, 100, 113, 258–9
    living in the basement 85–7
    mother's deterioration 89, 91–2
    near discoveries 83, 85, 91
    news of genocide from hotel staff 88–90
    radio reports 93–4
    saved by "French nationality" ruse 103–8, 114–5, 117–20, 128
    saved from threatened rape 113–5
    Vénuste (hotel waiter) 82–84, 115
host family in France 19, 130
humanitarian work 19–20, 42, 115–6, 141–2
loss of family members 17, 129–30
mixed heritage/ethnicity 22–3, 67, 81, 100
and mother 13, 19, 21, 31, 42, 44, 47, 55, 89, 91–2, 117, 121
pregnancy and parenthood 41–2, 46–7, 92
rescue and escape from Butare
    border encounter with *préfet* Nsabimana 128
    at Bujumbura refugee reception centre, Burundi 129–30
    help from François Pigeot 117–20
    at the Karubanda school, Butare 119–24
    mother held at gunpoint at Burundi border crossing 44, 47, 126–7
    recollection of convoy journey 56, 124–5
    separated and reunited with mother in Butare 117, 121
residual phobias/fears 92
saved photographs of life before the genocide 68–9
school education in France 19
school education in Rwanda 67–8, 103
teenage solace in reading 67–8
trials of the "Butare Six" 192–4
visits Michel Seine, veteran aid worker 174–8
Western imposed perspective/ interpretation of genocide archives 199–202, 238–53
see also Terre des Hommes
Umuhoza, Delphine 230–1, 236, 267
Umutoni, Claire "Fifi" 121, 164, 172, 209–14, 260

Union of Rwandan Industrialists 160
United Nations 49, 90–1, 93, 117, 127, 163, 188

V
Vanagt, Sarah 250
Vénuste (hotel waiter) 82–4, 115
Voice of America radio station 93, 103
VSD magazine 249

W
Wasungu, Willy 230–1
Wende, Tony 44, 49–50, 56, 131, 134, 200, 208, 217, 227, 239
Western journalistic perspective on genocide against the Tutsi 199–202, 238–53
Wieviorka, Annette 64
Wilkens, Carl 141
Winton, Nicholas 66

Z
Zaire 134, 142, 161, 163, 188–9, 247
Zwahlen, Ariane 145–6, 148–9